A Farewell to Farms

Reflections on a Transplanted Life

Douglas Howerton

For information about this title or to order other books
and/or electronic media, contact the author:

www.afarewelltofarmsbook.blogspot.com
email: douglashowerton13@gmail.com

Paperback ISBN: 979-8-218-59043-7

Printed in the United States of America

Book cover design and interior formatting: Van-Garde Imagery, Inc.

Disclaimer:
The narrative in this memoir reflects the author's recollection of
events. Some names have been changed to protect privacy. Dialogue
has been re-created from the author's memory. All topics of discussion
herein, including, but not limited to, relationships, domestic
abuse, education, employment, health and safety, and the effects of
alcoholism were presented for informational purposes and is not intended
as a substitute for professional advice.

For Mom and Dad
Thank you for life's invaluable lessons

Contents

Acknowledgements

First and foremost, I want to express my deepest gratitude to my family, whose love and support helped me navigate life's challenges and empowered me to pursue my goals.

I'd also like to give a big thank you to my partner, Brian Harpster for his unwavering support and encouragement throughout this writing journey. I am grateful for his insight, guidance and editing skills. His passion for literature has helped immensely in shaping this book.

A special thank you goes to my childhood friend Ryan for re-telling some of our adventures that I had forgotten about, and to my brothers Carl and David for sharing details of our upbringing.

I am indebted to Jack Headspeth for providing many historical details related to his father, Carroll Headspeth, and the role he played in preserving the history of our hometown, South Boston, VA.

A heartfelt thank you to Billy Wagner and my cousin Elizabeth Williamson for sharing some of the photographs within this book.

Finally, I want to thank all my friends (especially Anneke Mendiola) for their encouragement and support during this challenging but rewarding process.

Introduction

This memoir is a reflection of my journey as a child, and as an adult, raised in a small tobacco-farming community in Southern Virginia. It is a reflection of the trials, triumphs, dysfunction and stability of family life. It encompasses the camaraderie of best friends, our financial struggles, and our lack of opportunity. It embodies my desire to experience new things outside of what I perceived as mundane farm life. It is an elucidation of how I came to dislike living there, and how, now that I'm older, I have a desire to relive those days by writing down my history, recounting my parents' and grandparents' history, and participating in farm life discussions and recollections in online social media groups.

If history, specifically family history, is not retold, we lose our focal point for the past and the future. My purpose is to provide a description of this historical period in my life, and present a clearer perspective for current and future family members, and for interested readers outside of my family circle. I am fortunate to have such a diversified and endearing history. Each person has a different history. Some have a more interesting history than others, but the important thing is for your history to be preserved and shared.

Pen, Paper, Panic –
My Thoughts on Writing

Writing is hard work. I never knew writing was so strenuous until I took a writing class in college in 1998. I'd have an easier time digging a ditch than writing an essay, short story, or in this case my memoir. Although moving a pen across paper is not physically taxing, more sweat drips from my brow while writing than from digging. Why do I find writing such a strenuous activity?

For many years, my writing consisted of an occasional memo at work or letter home to Mom and Dad. My parents being simple folk, I'd tend to write simple letters. In my letters I'd describe the weather, my job, and maybe an infrequent trip. I'd often rehash memories of growing up, inquire about their health, and urge them to write back soon.

Writing an essay for a class at Cal State Fullerton meant finding new things to say and a new way to say them. Since I was not much of a reader in my younger days, except for newspapers and magazines, I found the essays that we read in class to be as strange as a foreign country. I'd read an assignment and the first thought that would come to mind would be, "How am I going to write a thousand-word essay on that?"

I'd stare at my writing tablet, begging my brain to come up with ideas. The blank sheets of paper mocked my effort. The coffee maker worked overtime. Crinkled papers containing exiled thoughts filled the trash bin to capacity! Eventually an idea would come forth. Like my letters home, my essays tended to incorporate family and personal incidents from the past. Writing about experiences gave me an entirely new range of ideas. From the innermost recesses of my brain, I excavated past experiences and memories, searching for topics. When one was found, it was as if a new vein of gold had been discovered, in a mine, years long abandoned.

When I finally had a topic, the next challenge was to put the topic into words. There are too many words in the English language, and too many choices. I would have a difficult time deciding which words to use. I'd get hung up on verb tenses and grammar usage. Punctuation became the bane of my existence!

When I took the writing class, I wanted to be a perfectionist and get things done right the first time. When I'd put a sentence down on paper, I wanted it to be cast in stone. However, these traits don't seem to be compatible with writing. As I write now, I'm constantly thinking of something to add, or some revision to make. Some days I end up revising what I've already written several times instead of moving forward with my story. But all the back and forth helps me gradually shape the whole piece into something that, hopefully, I'll be proud of.

My letters home to Mom and Dad changed after taking that class. I started to embellish my words and to make use of similes and metaphors. Instead of writing, "Not much new here," I'd write, "This week my life is as monotonous as peeling potatoes." Mom especially liked to read my letters. She was proud that I was getting a college education, experiencing new things, and seeing new places. My writing became her window to a world she had never experienced.

Now when I read, I look for words the author uses. I look at the way they construct sentences and formulate dialogue. When I'm finished writing my story, I'm going to rest my fatigued mind! If each sentence I've written is equivalent to lifting a shovel of dirt, I figure I've dug a ditch at least twenty feet long by now. It isn't a pointless endeavor; I've discovered the earth to be fertile, just perfect for a little self-growth!

Beginnings

I was born and raised in the mid-1950s in South Boston, Virginia, a small rural town of about 8,000 residents, on the banks of the Dan River, within the County of Halifax. I had an older brother (who has since passed), and have two younger brothers. We each were about two years apart in age. The following descriptions are a combination of history lessons taught in high school, word of mouth, and from personal experience:

Me, age six (1960)

South Boston is named after Boston, Massachusetts. It was formed in 1796 and incorporated as a town in 1884. It was originally called Boyd's Ferry and started out on the south side of the banks of the Dan River, in the area currently known as Riverdale. Due to flooding concerns, which remain today, the settlement was moved to the north side of the Dan River. There are many historic buildings in the downtown Main Street area. South Boston was a city until 1995; when population began to decline it then reverted back to town status.

Tobacco has always been a part of the history of South Boston and Halifax County. Tobacco was being grown in Virginia beginning in the early 1600s. In fact, according to historical records, the Native Americans were already growing tobacco when the first settlers arrived in Jamestown.

The National Tobacco Festival

Tobacco has been a major staple of the economy of Halifax County and the state of Virginia since 1700. Originating in 1935 in South Boston, the National Tobacco Festival was conceived by two local businessmen as a way to promote the superior quality of the local leaf. The first festival queen was Miss Westwood Byrd, daughter of the late Senator Harry Flood Byrd. Silent film star Mary Pickford led the festival in 1939. The three-day event featured pageants, parades, beauty queens, band competitions, clogging and fiddling contests, and Hollywood stunt men performing daring feats. It was attended by up to 100,000 people, including many celebrities. The last tobacco festival held in South Boston was in 1941; from there it moved to Richmond. (From the Library of Congress, American Folklife Center. Also published in *Virginia Living*, July 21, 2010).

Because of intense foreign competition, the average small-family farm like the one I grew up on has all but disappeared. The task of growing tobacco has been relegated to larger commercial farmers who deal directly with the tobacco companies. Smaller farms have more difficulty making a profit. From my observation, in the late 1970s and early 1980s there was a sharp decline in available labor needed to grow and process tobacco. Young people started heading off to college in order to avoid having to do manual labor. Farmers then resorted to hiring migrant labor. As a result of a combination of financial cost for supplies and labor, increased foreign competition, social attitudes toward the tobacco industry, and the end of the government tobacco price support program (the government guarantee that prices would not go below a certain level), growing tobacco had become a difficult venture for the poor or middle-class farmer.

There was a time when a few acres of tobacco could support a small family, but not anymore. There are still some large farms in Halifax County producing tobacco, but not nearly as many as when I was a child. These remaining farms grow tobacco and contract with the buyers directly. In the *old* days, cured tobacco was brought to a warehouse and auctioned off to the highest bidder. Many farmers stopped production of tobacco and a few tried hemp. At this time, hemp has mainly been too costly to produce, and only a few farms are growing it. There are also some seasonal farms which produce a wide variety of vegetables and fruit. Farmers Markets have also become very popular.

As property has been passed down from generation to generation, large tobacco farms that were once very productive are now being leased to outside power companies, which are installing hundreds of acres of solar panels on the land. In one particular area of the county known as *Clover*, a large swath of former farmland, almost 780 acres, contains 188,000 solar panels! (as reported in the June 28, 2024 issue of the local newspaper *The Gazette-Virginian*). In many instances, farms which had experienced regrowth of trees and other vegetation after the discontinuation of tobacco production have been bulldozed over for installation of these solar panels.

It's sad to think that this has happened to land that I actually worked on when tobacco crops were prevalent, land where I walked barefoot in the soil on hot summer days. It's also sad that wildlife is being displaced and the beauty of the landscape has been compromised. The issue has become very contentious, and many residents want a moratorium or a cap on the number of solar panel installations in the area; residents don't like the negative aesthetics and devaluation of their property. It remains to be seen what, if anything, will change.

When my family tended tobacco, we used land on my grandmother's farm, and we rented acreage from a family friend. The land that the family friend owned has now become a mobile home park. The beautiful, open and forested landscape is quickly being changed forever. With the loss of habitat, wildlife is being pushed out, especially birds. It's progress, but at what cost?

Downtown South Boston, VA

The downtown area has many historic brick buildings. I remember when there were dress shops, five-and-dime stores, men's shops, furniture stores, shoe stores, doctor's offices and even a historic hotel called the John Randolph (which is currently being refurbished). In the mid-1960s you could find almost anything you needed in Downtown South Boston. It was the place to be on Fridays and Saturdays! And on various occasions there were parades and marching bands from local high schools performing in the streets — most notable was the annual Christmas parade, which still takes place every year.

As far back as I can remember, which would be the early 1960s, South Boston was a vibrant center of the county. There was a large, three-story department store named Leggett's, where everyone went shopping on Fridays and Saturdays. I remember they had a basement floor called *the bargain basement*. Yep, that's where we shopped for shirts, jeans, shoes, etc., and where Mom bought all sorts of household goods, and fabric to make quilts. We liked Leggett's because they had a layaway plan. You pay a little, like a dollar a week, and pick up your items with the last payment.

There were also several drug stores. The ones I remember were Faulkner & Lawson's, Perkins Rexall and Reeves. Nowadays we call them pharmacies. I guess the term *drug store* has a certain negative connotation. The drug stores had soda fountains, and a counter with bar stools. One could order lunch or ice cream at the counter and wait for a prescription to be filled. The old historic drug stores were long ago replaced by large chain stores that sell merchandise, in addition to filling prescriptions.

When we went shopping in Downtown South Boston, we always saw someone we knew and would start up a conversation. Life was slow and laid-back. It's ironic how people seem to have had more time back then than they do now, yet today we supposedly have all the most modern conveniences helping us save time.

I remember a bicycle shop in the downtown area. As kids we would go in and look at the shiny new bikes. Our bikes were preowned that we had purchased at a bargain, or were put together from parts of other old bicycles: a chain from one, a wheel or handlebar from another. During a trip home from California in 1999, I remember meeting the former bicycle shop owner, Mr. Carroll Headspeth, at the Fine Arts Museum. It was about two years before he passed away in 2001.

Mr. Headspeth was 101 years old at the time I met him. I started up a conversation with him and learned that he was a local historian, so I asked if I could stop by his house for a chat before returning to California. He agreed, so I dropped by one afternoon and had a fascinating three-hour conversation with him about what life was like at the turn of the twentieth century, how he witnessed the changes in communication, farming, transportation, education and family life, from decade to decade, from about 1911 when he became a teenager until the day we had our discussion.

Mr. Headspeth recounted how Downtown South Boston had dirt streets. Transportation was primarily by horse and buggy and a few automobiles at the same time. He related stories of how cars would backfire and sometimes the bewildered horses would take off out of control down the street, and how that took some getting accustomed to!

He also recalled the covered bridge across the Dan River at South Boston that provided a means to cross the river in a north/south direction. He said that it was very rickety and noisy when wagons traveled across it, and that you could see the river through cracks in some of the boards. I remember as a kid walking across the newer bridge that replaced the old covered bridge. The boards on the walkway were broken in places, revealing the swirling and splashing water below. It was a very scary effort to get to the other side! A few years later, the walkway was cemented over. As of this writing, the pillars that supported the covered bridge are still visible in the river. They are made of smooth stones cemented together.

Mr. Headspeth also related that telephones were scarce in the early years of the twentieth century, especially in the rural areas. Usually, a country store near where people lived would have a phone. You'd have to turn a crank handle and ask the operator to ring the number you were calling.

Almost everyone he knew had some connection to farming, and a lot of the city businesses were geared towards supporting the farmer, especially the banks. Most people did not have the capital available to pay for equipment, supplies and labor in order to raise a tobacco crop, so they'd have to borrow money from the local bank and pay it back when the crop was sold. I asked the all-important question: "To what do you attribute your longevity?" His response was, "I take an aspirin a day, stay away from doctors and look both ways before crossing the street!" Great advice!

I had the opportunity very recently to talk with Mr. Headspeth's son Jack Headspeth. He related to me that his dad worked for a local South Boston newspaper until 1928, which was just before the Great Depression. The paper went out of business at that time, but he found a newspaper job in Westbury, NY and moved his family there until just before WW II started. He returned to South Boston in 1941 and managed the local Western Auto store until 1955 when he began operating Carroll's Auto. Mr. Headspeth served as local historian and also wrote three books related to the Civil and Revolutionary Wars.

On another visit to the Fine Arts Museum, I saw a collection of art from a local teacher and artist, Ms. Hedderly. She volunteered in some capacity at the Museum and I greatly admired her watercolor art. I was able to contact her and arrange a visit, much like the visit with the bicycle store owner. She painted many local scenes around Halifax County, depicting old tobacco barns, covered bridges, a railroad station, the County Courthouse and many more. I was able to buy several of her paintings and currently have them hanging in my home. The watercolor paintings were done in the 1970s and to my knowledge are no longer available.

Then there was Wilborn's Hardware, where everyone went for things like brooms, small appliances, and even garden and tobacco seeds. That building was torn down many years ago. My youngest brother (Carl) found someone who had the wood that used to be the countertops at Wilborn's. Carl obtained and repurposed the former countertops for a project in his home.

Next door to Wilborn's Hardware was Roses department store. Roses was a variety store, and as kids we would go there with our friends and get banana splits! They had a lunch counter, much like the drug stores in town, and balloons with a price tag inserted inside. You would pop the balloon and pay the price inside. We usually ended up paying almost the full price, which was ten or fifteen cents, no more than twenty-nine cents. Unfortunately, the Roses store was destroyed by a fire two days after Christmas in 1969. It was one of our favorite places to shop.

Like many small towns, there were barber shops and beauty salons, and even a shop called Eddie's Shoe Repair. Since we couldn't afford to buy new shoes every time they wore out, we'd go there and have new soles put on, or have other parts of the shoe repaired. It was a one-of-a kind business that, like other innovative businesses, ceased to exist because of changing times or needs.

The local fire department was also located in the downtown area next to the Newberry's five and dime store. In addition, there were appliance stores, dry cleaners, multiple old brick tobacco warehouses, several banks, a photo shop and even a taxi cab stand. The first large chain grocery store I remember going to when I was a child was the A & P store on Wilborn Avenue, the main thoroughfare north of downtown. At that time there were no barcodes on products. Grocery checkers had to punch all the prices in on a cash register for each item. The exciting thing about going to A & P back then was getting *green stamps* with every purchase. You could save them in a booklet and turn them in for various gifts. I still have one of the booklets of stamps, but the gifts have not been available for a long time.

After the major department store Leggett's moved to a shopping center just north of town, one by one the small shops that we had come to rely on disappeared. People started traveling to large malls in North Carolina for their needs. In addition, there weren't any restaurants in the downtown area that would attract locals or tourists. As was common in a lot of old downtown areas of the country, a few antique stores moved in, but that was short-lived. South Boston was a town where you could do one-stop shopping. We could shop for clothes, shoes, garden seeds, and even appliances. The library and post office were, and still are, within walking distance of the downtown area. Other services such as banks and insurance were also located there. Nowadays we all tend to drive longer distances and spend more time locating goods and services.

South Boston was a small tight-knit farming community. The town's prosperity was inextricably intertwined with the fortunes of the farmers. If the farmers prospered then so would the businesses. If the crops failed, the businesses would suffer. This is what ultimately happened in the 1980s and 1990s. With the decline of farming and also the demise of the textile industry, many stores eventually closed down.

Fast forward to the early 2000s and the area has seen a lot of revitalization. Buildings are being repurposed, mainly as restaurants, although there are still some merchandising businesses there as well. People are now gravitating back to the old downtown. The town is promoting tourism more than ever. This is true in many areas of the country.

The old downtown tobacco warehouse district has been revitalized, and several buildings now house a large Continuing Education Center. Local students can obtain a wide range of degrees through both on-line and on-site courses with major universities. This center is seen as a huge re-educational need in a community that had lost most of the major employers in the textile, plastics, furniture and shoe making industries. These industries provided employment for countless numbers of residents since the early 1930s, or before.

Almost every family that I knew in the 1960s worked in one of those industries until the late 1990s early 2000s when most of the manufacturing in the area went overseas due to cheaper labor. All my family, including myself, worked in textiles as well as tobacco farming. I worked at J.P. Stevens, the local textile mill, for thirteen years.

One of Downtown South Boston's renovated buildings is called The Prizery. As described on www.prizery.org:

> Renovation began in 2002, and the facility includes a performing arts theatre, art gallery, classrooms, and a large rental space for community functions. Today the Prizery plays host to performers from throughout the world in the 250-seat Chastain Theatre, exhibits art in the Robert F. Cage Art Gallery, provides venues for events and rentals, and makes a wide range of classes available — from music to art. The building was originally where tobacco was 'prized,' or pressed layer by layer into hogshead barrels often weighing up to 1,000 pounds. After the autumn harvest, the plants were first 'stemmed,' or stripped of fibers and then packed. The barrels were then taken down to the river or the railroad for shipping. (www.*prizery.org*, "About the Prizery", 2024).

Many theatre and musical productions are now being performed there. To date, this venue has brought a lot of cultural events to the local community, cultural events that did not exist when I lived there.

Berry Hill Plantation (circa 1835-1840)
from the Library of Congress photos

Berry Hill Plantation

There is no shortage of historic, nineteenth-century homes in and around Downtown South Boston. Just a few miles from downtown, on the River Road, is the crown jewel of Halifax County: Berry Hill Resort and Conference Center.

From our history lessons in high school, I learned that the Berry Hill mansion, completed in 1844, contained seventeen rooms and a great entrance hall. According to the National Register of Historic Places:

> James Coles Bruce inherited from his father, a tract of land which was once owned by William Bryd of Westover. On this land stood a red brick house with two principal outbuildings. Bruce had the house transformed (circa 1839) into one of the greatest Greek Revival mansions in the country (…) The great octastyle portico of the house was based on that of the Parthenon. ("Halifax County's Timeless Treasure: Berry Hill Resort," *Hyco Lake Magazine*, Boatwright, Phyllis, September 16, 2013).

In the 1970s and 1980s, I would occasionally drive the River Road where Berry Hill is located, and could barely get a glimpse of the mansion. It sits a half-mile off the main road. My friends had always told me it was haunted, and that they had on several occasions seen a light in one of the windows. However, I did not get that impression when

I visited the property several years ago. I inquired of the tour guide if they had noticed any unusual occurrences there, and was told that there were tales of footsteps being heard, faucets turning on by themselves and guests' shoes moving around on their own. Some people claim to have taken photographs that have *orbs* of light in them.

Berry Hill has been bought and sold a few times over the years. The tour guide informed us that a French insurance agency purchased the property in the late 1980s for use as a training center, and added the hotel and over 5,000 square feet of indoor meeting space. The mansion is currently a family-owned resort that has become a popular wedding venue, and hosts many different retreats as well as the annual Virginia Cantaloupe Festival each July. Here's a description from *Hyco Lake Magazine*:

> At one time there were about 200 slaves, living on the property, who worked crops of tobacco, corn, wheat, oats, and hay. They also tended livestock. There are remains of the slave quarters throughout the property. When emancipation occurred, many of the former slaves remained at Berry Hill as paid workers, because their owner, James Coles Bruce had been kind to them. The property currently houses two restaurants, a conference center and guest rooms. Other amenities include an indoor pool, basketball, tennis and pickleball courts, saunas, walking trails, and historical tours. ("*Halifax County's Timeless Treasure: Berry Hill Resort*," Hyco Lake Magazine, Boatwright, Phyllis, September 16, 2013).

Childhood Adventures

I was a kid in the 60s, and we basically invented games to play, like *King of the Hill* and *Kick the Can*. We didn't have video games back then and we couldn't afford things like train sets or board games. Our best friends Ronnie and Ryan (who were twins) lived just a short distance from us. I don't remember how we met, although it was probably at the small country store adjacent to where we lived. We were always running in and out of that store for candy, sodas, chips and bubble gum. We probably met around 1960 when I was in first grade. We all attended the same elementary school and our parents knew each other. Our parents and their parents worked at the same local textile mill, and in a small town such as ours, everyone knew everyone else.

There's no way to sum up the number of days we spent together, how many adventures we experienced, how similar our two family's upbringing was, how many ball games we attended, how many miles we rode our bikes each day, or how many conversations and experiences we shared over the years. We developed a bond, a close friendship that has lasted more than sixty years! Although we now live almost three thousand miles apart, we still phone, text and write to each other.

Ronnie was tall, lanky and mostly quiet, like myself. Ryan was shorter, with a more of a stocky build, and always the prankster in the group! He was always (and still does) pulling a prank on the rest of our group. We never knew what he was up to. Both were always very competitive with each other. Sometimes resentment flared between them over which one was born first, but they cared very much for each other, and family was, and is, extremely important to them.

My brother David and our dog Stonie (mid-1960s) on the "Dump" road

Our group consisted of Ronnie and Ryan, who were the oldest, myself, one year younger than the twins, and my brothers David (two years younger) and Carl (four years younger than myself). The twins were always the leaders in the group and my brothers and myself followed along. We had an abiding affection for them. We all grew up poor, and we all had to work hard as kids. We didn't get a lot of the material things that kids get nowadays. Our friendship has stood the test of time.

We respected our elders, and we were disciplined when we exhibited bad behavior. If we talked back to our parents or didn't complete chores given to us, we'd get the dreaded *switch* treatment! A switch was a small branch from a bush or tree. My dad would whip us with it and we'd end up with red whelps on our legs.

When we weren't working in tobacco or doing chores, we spent our free time roaming the woods with our two dogs, Brownie and Stonie. Brownie was a mixed Hound and Shepherd, and Stonie was full German Shepherd. They went with us everywhere during the early 60s to the early 70s. In the country, a boy almost always had a family dog tagging along, up and down country roads, dirt roads that led to the tobacco field and the creek, or just rambling through the woods.

As long as I can remember, we always had a dog in the family. Our dogs stayed outside, even in the cold winters, except for the Chihuahuas. The outside dogs were able to get inside the old tobacco pack house at night, or slept on the back porch.

There were cats too -- lots of them. They also stayed outside, and did a good job of keeping the rat population down. Mom had a favorite cat named Nellie Belle. She too was an outside cat who roamed during the day and slept in the old pack house in their back yard at night. Nellie Belle lived to be sixteen years old. In the spring of 2010, Mom found her deceased early one morning in the backyard after a bad rainstorm. It appeared that Nellie may have been ill and had been headed towards Mom's house for help at the time. It was devastating for Mom to lose Nellie Belle; she did not have anymore cats after this loss.

Mom used to get so exasperated with us when our friends came to visit! We never stopped to sit down and have lunch when we were exploring, instead we'd run in and out of the house during the day looking for snacks. Our house opened up to the backyard, and there were steep wooden steps leading up to the kitchen entrance. We'd run up and down the steps, grabbing peanut butter crackers and Kool-Aid, and run back outside again. We were poor, so that was our lunch! I know we must have been annoying, and I'm surprised that Mom didn't lock the door! On numerous occasions, I remember Mom saying, "Ya'll either stay in or out!"

Our yard was full of color and the pleasant sounds of spring. During springtime, birds were busy building nests and singing. We had cardinals, bluejays, brown thrashers, robins, mockingbirds and sparrows, just to name a few. There was a menagerie of colors that came alive at this time of year. Mom had irises, gladiolas, forsythia, roses, and her prized azaleas, as well as white-flowering dogwoods and redbuds. The night air was filled with the intoxicating fragrance of honeysuckle, and wild blackberries were abundant in the edges of the woods. Their white blooms gave the appearance of snow from a distance. Spring was when the angle of the sun cast ghostly silhouettes of the newly sprouted leaves on the yard and the forest floor. The leaves were not yet big enough to block out the sun and produce shade. Instead, they created a dazzling, shadowy display of light.

Grape Vines, Barbed Wire and Ghosts

On one occasion, us kids decided to follow the creek from the point where it crossed Grandmother's property over to the next owner's property. We discovered lots of minnows in that section of the creek, and we would come back occasionally to *sand* the creek bed with a makeshift trap, constructed of a burlap bag nailed to two sticks. We'd catch the minnows and use them as fish bait at our local pond.

At that part of the creek, we saw lots of long grapevines hanging from the tops of trees. Some of them must have been as big around as our arms. They were sturdy enough that we could swing on them and go sailing through the air landing on the other side of the creek! There was also a tree with a canopy of grapevines so thick that we could climb up and actually sit on top of the canopy.

Once, when we were in that section of the neighbor's woods in the late afternoon, we heard a strange growling noise and saw shadows that seemed to be moving on the hill above the creek. I was the first one to start running! We couldn't really see where we were going; we were just running as fast as we could. I ran into a barbed wire fence and a piece of the fence broke and hit me just below the eyebrow. I ended up with a gash, but never went to see a doctor. It was very common in those days not to see a doctor for things like that, even though I probably should have had a few stitches. My friends' mom patched me up and we just kept going. I still have the scar today!

A few years later, I related this story to my grandmother, and she told me that she had heard that Native Americans lived in the area at one time, and according to local folklore, there was a burial ground in the area where we had found the grapevines and had heard the growling noises. In fact, history does record that there were tribes of Native Americans who lived in Halifax County at one time. It makes one wonder if the spirits of the past were active in that area. Or maybe it could have been a bear or some other animal. In any event, from that time forward, we never visited that section of creek with the huge grapevines anymore, and we never heard those noises again.

There were other strange things that happened at night. Our two dogs stayed outside at night, and I remember when I was about twelve years old being abruptly awakened by loud barking and growling in the early morning hours. I got up and turned on the back porch light and there was a pack of six wild dogs trying to attack our dogs. I'd never heard of a pack of wild dogs, but they weren't wolves or coyotes. They looked just like ordinary dogs. I yelled at them and they ran off. I never saw or heard them anymore after that incident. One of our friends related a story about walking home from visiting his girlfriend, during which he encountered a similar pack of wild dogs on the outskirts of the city. He said he just kept walking and they didn't bother him.

We didn't have cell phones back then, and pay phones were only available close to businesses, so there was no way to get someone to help you if you needed to. I think that living in an isolated area with no outside lighting gives rise to more unexplained noises and incidents such as these, and lends to a more vivid imagination! We did not usually lock our doors at night in the country, but after experiencing these incidents, I made sure they were locked before going to bed!

Favorite Games and Toys

One of our favorite games was *marbles*. We started by drawing a circle in the dirt of our yard, and placing about twenty marbles in the circle. We'd take turns *thumping* the marbles out of the circle with another marble between our thumb and index finger. If one person didn't move a marble out of the circle, then the next person tried. Whoever knocked the most marbles out of the circle was the winner.

Jack rocks was another popular game that we played as kids in the 1960s. We usually had three players at a time, and we'd sit on the floor in a circle, and then scatter ten jacks on a flat surface. A rubber ball was tossed in the air and you had to pick up one jack and catch the ball after the first bounce. In round two, you'd have to throw the ball in the air and pick up two jacks after the first bounce. We continued each round until the jacks were all picked up. The person with the most jacks was the winner.

We didn't usually get toys for Christmas. Our gifts consisted mostly of practical things like clothes or shoes. The exception to this was when the textile mill where Dad worked at had their annual Christmas party. All the families came with their kids to these parties, and the management handed out bags of fruit and toys. Sometimes there were board games, toy soldiers, flutes, yo-yos and paddle balls. It was an exciting time for us!

When springtime arrived in Southern Virginia, usually in late March or early April, we finally got the last vestiges of winter. The cold, blustery north winds gave way to gentle spring breezes and warm sunny days. Perfect kite flying days! Neither my friends nor my brothers and I could afford a fancy store-bought kite, although occasionally we'd get a real kite for Christmas.

My brother Carl and our dog Brownie in our back yard (mid-1960s)

In the early 1960s, dry cleaners used giant paper bags to cover garments waiting to be picked up. Whenever we found someone who had a dry cleaner bag, we used the bags to make our own kites. We'd trim very small tree branches and use twine to tie them together in a triangle shape, and then cut the bag and tape it to the sticks. We'd get Mom to give us some scrap material to make a tail. Sometimes these homemade kites would fly for a while, but usually what happened is that the wind would take them down rather quickly! The paper was really too thin for a kite. No matter, we had fun trying!

We also played with plastic toy soldiers. We'd set up a battlefield in the dirt. We had soldiers, tanks and artillery. Each person was allowed to make a battle move, and the others a counter move. Whoever had the most soldiers and equipment at the end of the game won.

In 1972 I was close to graduating from high school and the Vietnam War was still going on. I remember taking a Psychology class and hearing the teacher ask if we thought that playing toy soldiers as a child helped create a dangerously romantic image of war and combat for many young boys and men in this period. I believe it's possible, and I think some boys may have also become more of a bully because of it, but I don't think that my friends or myself ever romanticized war. In fact, we were genuinely afraid of being called for duty. I registered for the draft, and was out of high school three years before the war ended. Luckily none of my friends or myself were called up. My brother David was a conscientious objector, and I obtained the necessary forms and helped him complete them. He was granted that status and was not drafted.

Left to right: The Howerton brothers Richard, Douglas, David and Carl (1964)

The old pond where we fished and ice skated

The Old Windshield, Frozen Ponds, and Huts

My brothers, myself, and our friends were notorious for getting into things that we shouldn't have! I remember one particular winter when we were sledding down the hill from the tobacco barn at my grandparent's house. In the 1960s people didn't take their trash or discarded junk items to a landfill. If you lived in the country, as we did, you tossed unwanted items in a *gulley*, which was like a wide ditch in the woods. No one gave environmental issues or pollution a second thought back then like they do today. On that particular day, we found an old discarded car windshield in the gulley close to where we were sledding. My friend Ryan remarked, "This would make a great sled!"

We carried the windshield up to the top of the hill by the old tobacco barn and started sliding down the hill in the snow. It went fast! A lot faster than a sled. Little did we know that had we hit a rock or slid into a tree, the glass could have broken and cut us, or we could have been thrown off and injured. Mom had been visiting Grandma, and she heard our excited voices and came to investigate. She was so angry with us for not realizing the danger. Kids just don't think about hazards when they're having a good time. Mom took the windshield, threw it against a big rock, and it shattered into a thousand pieces! And that was the end of our sledding adventure!

So we lost our perfect sled, but not to worry. We just moved on to another adventure. We had friends who lived just down the road from us, and we hung around together whenever we could. There was a pond behind their house and we'd go fishing there in the spring and summer. If we caught fish we'd bring them home for Mom to fry in a cast iron skillet (Dad would only eat fish if they were battered in cornmeal and fried).

It wasn't until we were in our mid-to-late teens that we were able to buy a fancy fishing pole or a *rod and reel*. With the rod and reel, we could cast the line all the way to the middle of the pond. When we were nine or ten years old, we made our own fishing poles, which were straight, young saplings trimmed down so they were smooth. We just attached a nylon line, a cork and a sinker to the end of the pole. We could usually buy the basics at our local country store. For bait, we dug up worms behind the old tobacco pack house, or caught minnows in the creek near Grandma's house. I liked fishing the first few times I went, but for me, it never developed into a long-term sport or pastime. On the other hand, my childhood friends still fish on a regular basis.

When we were kids, the pond would freeze over almost every winter; we had the perfect ice-skating rink right in our back yard! We wore our regular shoes and just got a running start from the shore and slid as far across as we could. Our moms were too far away to hear us if we got into trouble though. I remember one time we were skating and the ice cracked open where my oldest brother was skating. He fell through the ice and was in water up to his knees. Luckily it wasn't deep, otherwise he would have been in trouble. We learned not to go very far out on the pond, and in fact, when Mom found out about it, we were forbidden to go to the pond unless an adult was with us

Our friend Ryan related a story not long ago in which he and his brother, and some other friends, were at the pond one day, and Ryan decided to play a joke on his mom. He started yelling that his brother had fallen in the water and was drowning! Their house was fairly close to the pond, so his mom could hear him and she ran down to the pond to help. When she found out that he was joking, Ryan got the whipping of his lifetime, either with a belt or a switch.

That pond is still there, but I understand from talking to my brothers that it never freezes over in the winter anymore. Winters there are much warmer now than when we were kids. Maybe a result of climate change and global warming? In January and February we would typically have several days of sub-freezing temperatures. So, what did we do when we couldn't go to the pond and skate? Another dangerous activity of course! We took our sled onto the paved road and took turns pushing each other, until a car came down the street or Mom or Dad yelled at us through an open window. I haven't seen the pond since I was in my teens, but I've seen recent pictures. I would imagine that there are a lot of fish in that pond by now, but the snowy and icy days of our childhood have long since disappeared.

Another thing we did at the pond was to construct huts out of fallen tree branches, fresh pine boughs and wild straw called *broom sage* that grew in nearby open fields. Grandma used to pick the same wild straw and make brooms out of it. She related to me that this was the only type of broom their family had until sometime in the early 1960s. We built the huts on the edge of a deep ravine which was the overflow drain for the pond. We sometimes would get a running start and jump across to the other side. It's a wonder that we were never seriously injured from doing that. The huts were our hiding places. We'd bring snacks from home or go to the little country store and buy junk food. This was where we'd plan our next adventure. Sometimes we'd have mud ball contests to see if we could knock down the other person's hut. Not long after we built the huts, a big rain storm came and blew them over. We never tried to rebuild them after that.

There was another pond on a neighbor's property near one of our tobacco fields. We sometimes visited there after finishing our work, and would often wade into the water to cool off. I remember getting into the water with my oldest brother and his best friend Frankie one hot summer day. We were about halfway out to the middle of the pond when I stepped into a hole unexpectedly and went underwater. I remember panicking and clinging to my brother's shoulders to stay afloat! After this incident and to this day, I have been wary of large bodies of water.

Halloween

As a kid in the 1960s we didn't have much, so when Halloween rolled around, we almost could not contain our excitement! The problem was that there were no Halloween stores where you could buy a nice costume, so we made our own. They were very basic, such as Cowboys and Indians. Our costumes consisted of jeans, an old hat, and a cap pistol strapped to our sides. Living in the country, the houses were so far apart that it wasn't worth it to trick or treat there, so we walked all the way to town, which was about two to three miles. Our two friends that we hung around with moved to the city in the mid-1960s, so we'd meet up at their house, put on our costumes and go out, hoping for a big haul of candy! We usually came back with bags full! I remember there were kids older than us who'd put firecrackers inside pumpkins that people had on their porches, ending up with a mess all over their porch. There were other kids who vandalized mailboxes with cherry bombs. Sometimes the older kids got into a lot of trouble at Halloween including injuries from explosives. When we were done trick-or-treating, we usually spent the night with our friends and walked home the next day. We'd have enough candy to last for weeks!

The Creek

Summer days were hot with seemingly unending, unbearable humidity. Sunrises spilling over the early morning horizon set the woods ablaze with the bright red and yellow of daybreak. After a morning storm, the sky was a canvas of bright colors. The sun became a profusely bright-yellow ball, casting eerie shadows onto the forest floor as we went about our day. After being outside for literally five minutes, our clothes would be drenched with sweat! Summer nights weren't much better, but we did have a very old, round metal fan that fit in the window. That fan must have been a survivor of the 1930s or 1940s! It was very noisy and rattled like it might fall apart any minute. As soon as I thought my brothers were asleep, I'd turn the fan towards me. One of my brothers would always wake up and turn the fan on them. What usually happened is that we'd argue about who should have the fan on them, and then Mom would come and unplug it! We would have thunderstorms quite often at night and our parents would not allow us to run the fan during a storm. That's when it got really miserable inside.

During the summer there were lots of unusual sounds at night. Periodically there were cicadas which made loud buzzing noises when they emerged from the ground. There were also crickets, and there were whippoorwills, which were small brown birds in the forests that sang at night. In late March and early April, mockingbirds also sang in the middle of the night. All of this non-stop buzzing and singing was primarily to attract a mate.

After our work in tobacco and chores around the house were finished, we would go to the creek to cool off from the constant 90-degree heat and drenching humidity, or we'd go fishing at our local pond. To get to the creek, we had to walk about a mile down a steep dirt road filled with trenches washed out from thunderstorms, through a pine forest and cross the creek at its shallow spot. There was a huge hill on both sides. Looking up from the creek, the surrounding area looked as if we were in the mountains. Since we took this route to get to one field of tobacco near the creek, my dad had constructed a small wooden bridge, just wide enough for the tractor and trailer we used, to bring tobacco plants, fertilizer, water and insecticide to use on the crop. We also used this bridge to cross the creek. We'd walk along its bank until we came to the deepest point and take turns jumping in. We didn't have swim trunks, so we *skinny dipped*. On one occasion, I remember seeing a water moccasin snake in the water, but even that didn't deter us. It's funny, when we were kids, we didn't have a heightened sense of danger. We were more interested in just having fun! Most of the time our two dogs, Brownie and Stonie, would also get in the water, but in the shallowest part. We'd play in the water for a couple of hours and then head back home.

On the way home from the creek, we'd sometimes walk through freshly plowed fields in search of Native American arrowheads. When we were kids, it was common to find these, especially near creeks or rivers. Over the years, we found a few; with the passage of time, they have long since been misplaced or lost.

Entertainment

Our television had rabbit ears for an antenna and only three or four channels. I remember watching the show *Dark Shadows* in the mid-1960s. I would rush in from school and watch it before I did anything else. Mom used to admonish us for watching such a dark, gothic soap opera, but I remember being enthralled by vampires and witches, and then I couldn't sleep at night! Eventually, Mom stopped us from watching *Dark Shadows* when I was about twelve years old. After I moved to California, I found the series on a cable channel and *binge watched* every episode, all 1,225 of them, over the course of a few months!

We didn't have our own video games, and cell phones were not yet in existence. Our parents most likely would not have allowed us to have electronic devices even if they had existed at the time. The distractions that come with them would have prevented us from doing our work. Of course, there were a few video games, such as Pac Man or Pin Ball at the only bowling alley in town. The bowling alley was located in Hupp's Mill Plaza Shopping Center, across from the hospital.

The shopping center is named after a grist mill. It was called Hupp's Mill and was located directly across the street from the plaza. It was built in 1855 and was owned and operated by Daniel Hupp from 1881 until the early 1920s. There were new owners from the 1920s until fire destroyed the building in 1942. However, they kept the *Hupps Mill* name. "Old Iron Wheel Is All That's Left of Hupp's Mill," *South Boston*

News, January 12, 1960, p. 2., and from my 1999 interview with local historian Carroll Headspeth.

There was also a pool hall in the downtown area, but we weren't allowed in there. Shady people hung out there, and alcohol use was common. There was only one movie theater on North Main Street in town. It was called the Princess Theatre back in the 1930s and was a popular place for young people to go. I remember going there in my junior year of high school to see the movie *Romeo and Juliet* with a group of high school English students. Seeing the movie was part of our grade, and I remember having to write a short paper. That was the only movie I ever saw there. In recent years, the theater has been sitting idle, due to the prohibitive costs to refurbish it. Nowadays there is an outdoor screen near the old downtown warehouse district which has periodic movie events.

In the early 1970s there was a small business near town called Duffy's where teenagers hung out and played pool. I was four years older than my youngest brother, Carl who frequented the place on the weekends. One night I made the mistake of buying beer for Carl and a group of his underaged teen friends. A State Police officer was watching my car and pulled in beside me. He threatened to arrest me unless I poured the beer out on the ground, which I happily did! I never went to that place anymore, and never purchased alcohol for underaged kids anymore after that incident. Sometimes lessons are learned the hard way! Had I been arrested the story would have been front-page news in the *Everyday Life* section of the local paper. I would have been ostracized, or maybe even banished from the community!

Mom

It's really difficult to put into words how much my mom meant to me. She had a hard upbringing. She endured hardships that would sink the average person. She was the one constant and unchanging presence in my life, the stability that held us together as a family. She never gave up in the face of whatever adversities were thrown her way.

Mom was born in 1929, at the start of the Great Depression. She never knew anything but work. She never saw a concert or play. She never visited the ocean or flew on a plane, although she talked about it often. She never learned how to drive. Most of the things we take for granted she never got to experience. When I learned how to drive and got my first car at age eighteen, I would take Mom and her younger sister Laura to visit their other sister Thelma and her husband in Richmond, Virginia. Most of the time my grandma came with us.

I would also take Mom, Aunt Laura and Grandma to see Mom's brother and his family in North Carolina. For the next eighteen years I made sure Mom got to see all her family, and went wherever she wanted or needed to go.

As I recall Mom describing her childhood, she finished the seventh grade and dropped out soon after starting the eighth grade. Her family moved around from farm to farm as sharecroppers in order to find work. It was difficult for Mom to keep changing schools. She also mentioned that some of her female classmates wore makeup and fancy clothes. Mom never had these things when she was in school. One hears lots of hardship stories that occurred during the Great Depression, and Mom's family had plenty of them.

The remnants of Mom's birth home in 2016 (built circa 1920's)
Aarons Creek, Halifax County, VA

One thing that stands out in my mind is the fact that she wore dresses made out of feed sacks to school. Feed suppliers used colorful materials during the Depression to make their feed sacks because they knew that poor people were reusing them for clothing and quilts. Mom's classmates would poke fun at her because of the type of clothing she wore and her lack of makeup. In fact, she never wore any makeup her entire life. She didn't need it because she had natural beauty! This was one of the reasons that she didn't want to continue with school, because of the bullying.

I had a conversation with Mom sometime in 2008 or 2009 and asked her what was it like when she was dating my dad in 1949. She told me that my dad came around looking for work, so my grandpa hired him to pull tobacco plants from the plant beds and help transplant them out into the fields. That's how they met. He kept coming around and eventually they started doing things together. At the time, young people who were dating usually sat in the parlor or living room with a chaperone present, usually one of the girl's parents. Dad didn't have a car at the time, so he borrowed my grandpa's mule and they rode the mule about two miles to the crossroads community of Riverdale, which is within sight the downtown area of my hometown of South Boston. They had some food, and then came back home. This was her first date! Later on, Dad bought an old 1951 Ford coupe and they'd go to see movies in town or visit his family. Not the whirlwind, app-driven dating of the twenty-first century for sure! I still have a picture of that old car with my brothers and myself standing next to it.

Mom married my dad in 1950 when she was twenty-one years old and he was twenty. For a short time she worked at the local textile mill, but had to stop when my brother Richard was born in 1951. From that time forward she was a full-time homemaker. For the most part in the 1950s, women stayed home, had babies, and kept house. That was the stereotypical role that was expected of them. In some circles nowadays, it is thought that we might be headed back in that direction in our country.

Although Mom never finished high school, she was great at writing, English and math. She was the Chief Financial Officer of our household. She managed to save money from my dad's earnings at the local Esso gas station, enough money so that they were able to build two additional rooms onto their two-room home. She was also able to pay for life insurance policies for each family member. Back then, insurance agents made home calls to collect insurance premiums. In lieu of a receipt, the agent gave Mom a small booklet in which to record each payment. I remember her searching for change to pay the agent. Somehow, she was able to meet all our financial obligations.

Grandpa Newton top left, Mom to the right of him (circa 1949). Seventh-Day Adventist Church family

Every year Mom grew sweet potato plants from full-size potatoes she put in a ground bed. She would stake a sign in the front yard saying, "Sweet Potato Plants for Sale." I remember the variety she liked best was called *maple leaf*. She'd make enough to pay a bill here and there, or buy something we needed.

I also remember Mom being an avid gardener. She could take cuttings of plants, propagate them, and grow full size plants of all sorts. Her favorite flowers were purple irises, azaleas, roses and forsythia (golden bell). Every spring the yard was filled with vibrant colors. There were also maple, dogwood, red bud and crepe myrtle trees which added more color in the spring and fall.

*Left to right: My brothers David, Richard, myself and Carl
in front of Dad's 1951 Ford*

*Myself, brothers David, Richard and Carl with Aunt Laura, and
"Sparkie" (circa 1960)*

Mom also looked forward to planting a large vegetable garden each spring. We planted tomatoes, corn, squash, butterbeans, snap beans, peas and turnip greens. When we harvested vegetables, there were literally bushels of produce. We also grew a large field of corn and potatoes, and a *sallet patch*. We called turnip greens *sallet*. Mom either canned or froze literally hundreds of containers of everything we grew each year. She also had an old Damson plum tree in the back yard, along with peach, apple and pear trees. She'd make jelly or preserves out of the fruit. It was a long hard summer, preserving food, working in tobacco, housekeeping and wrangling finances, but somehow, she managed. Of course, us kids helped with picking the vegetables and shelling beans and peas. Mom had a makeshift barbecue in the back yard where she could cook big pots of vegetables or can jars of tomatoes or snap beans. I remember helping her keep the wood fire going.

Mom in the garden behind Grandma's smoke house (early 1960s)

Mom cooked wonderful meals! They were mostly simply-prepared food from the garden that country folk ate. During the summer we'd have lunchtime meals of fried squash and onions, green beans, corn, tomatoes, homemade biscuits and blackberry cobbler. These were all things we grew in the garden, or with blackberries, picked in the wild. Sometimes, especially in colder months, we'd have a pot of October beans, Purple Hull peas or butterbeans, and pan-fried cornbread. Our cornbread was made using white corn meal mixed with a little butter-milk and cooked in a hot, greased cast-iron skillet. There was always dessert too! Usually a chocolate, sweet potato or coconut pie. Banana pudding was my favorite!

Mom, my brother David, and dog Stonie in our back yard (1966)

We seldom ate meat. Sometimes we had meatloaf, chicken, or turkey at Thanksgiving or Christmas, but most days there was no meat. We were vegetarians the rest of the year.

Mom always made sure we had everything we needed for school, and that we spent enough time doing our homework. My oldest brother (Richard) and next to youngest brother (David) never finished high school. They had other ideas, and it was a struggle to get them out of bed in the morning and off to school. They skipped many classes, or went to school but didn't pay attention. When they were old enough they dropped out altogether. I was the first in my family to graduate from high school, and my youngest brother (Carl) finished four years later. I was disappointed that my dad didn't go to either ceremony. I was the only one who later went on to college.

Our home (1950). The right half dates to 1972

Mom was always there to help us, and we could always approach her if we needed assistance. She was the one who sat up with us at night when we were sick, patched us up when we got hurt, and helped us when we needed direction in our school work. Our lives were intertwined and inseparable. She had her faith to draw upon and help her through the rough times, especially with Dad's drinking problem.

Mom was a Seventh-Day Adventist. She took all of us kids with her to church every Saturday until we got older and some of us decided that we didn't want to go any longer. She and Grandma continued to attend when the kids stopped going. For a time, I attended a local Baptist church but it turned out not to be an all-inclusive environment, and after a while I stopped attending. Mom was active in her church, always helping some friend or church family that needed assistance. She loved gospel music and country/bluegrass music. Years after I had moved to California, we organized a little music festival in my brother's front yard. It was around 2012. There was guitar playing, singing and food. Many of her neighbors attended. Mom had suffered a stroke in 2010 and we brought her from the convalescent home to my brother's house. I remember how much she enjoyed it. It was an occasion we will all remember fondly.

Mom and her azaleas in 2010

Mom was a quiet person. She loved solving word-search and crossword puzzles. She didn't talk much unless she was upset about something. Most of us kids were the same way. We could sit together for long periods of time and not say a word, but it was the unsaid things that mattered, the fact that we stood up for each other. And we could always talk about our problems if we needed to.

Home Life

I respected Mom and Dad. Even though I didn't always agree with them, I appreciated the fact that they were there to take care of us. I did not feel as close to my dad as I did to Mom. She was always there when we needed her, but a lot of the time Dad wasn't. Mom would comment to her friends that the best thing that ever happened to her was having her four children. We stood up for her when she needed it, just like she did for us when we were kids. When our dad drank and became belligerent, we would sometimes have to stand between the two of them to avoid a fight. In that respect, we were very protective of her. She deserved the best of everything, but it didn't always work out that way. Still, she got the love of her children.

My parents got married in 1950. They first lived with my paternal grandmother, Willie Howerton. There were seven of my dad's siblings in the house, plus my parents and my grandmother. This soon became unbearable, and I remember Mom saying that if they didn't find a place of their own soon, she was going back home to live with her parents. My dad found an old building in back of a neighbor's farm, on Hyco Road, about a mile south of where us kids were raised. The property was owned by a wealthy couple whose family came from England in the early 1800s. The building was a converted chicken coop. There was one room that served as bedroom, kitchen and living room. My mom said that the ceiling was so low that you had to bend over slightly when inside. Of course there was no bathroom, but there was a Johnny House out back. Still, this was preferable to living with seven other people.

When they married, Grandma Newton gave each of her four children an acre of land on which to build their own home. I recently found the original deed where my grandma gifted an acre of land to Mom in 1952. That's when she had the original two rooms of their home built. While living in the converted chicken coop, Mom hired a local contractor friend to construct a two-room house. Originally there was a kitchen and one bedroom. The kitchen also served as a living room. There was a small gas stove for cooking and a freestanding porcelain sink for washing dishes.

There was no running water when they first moved into the new house. Mom related to me that when she first moved in she had to carry buckets of water from my grandma's well. Grandma lived within sight of Mom's new place, but it was a trek. The well had two buckets attached to a chain that traveled over a pully. You lowered an empty bucket into the well, and pulled the full bucket up. The water was cold and refreshing, especially on a hot muggy summer day! Grandma kept a bucket of the water and a dipper on a table on her back porch. Everyone who visited her drank from the same dipper, and to my knowledge, never became sick from doing so.

Later on, my parents had their own well with an electric pump. Still, Mom had to carry the water inside in buckets. Clothes were washed in the sink. Baths were done by heating water and pouring it in the sink and taking a sponge bath, or filling a large, round galvanized metal tub, like the ones you see people planting flowers in nowadays. Each one of us kids took a turn in the bath water. For heat in the wintertime, there was a small tin wood heater with a stove pipe attached to a cinderblock chimney in the kitchen. Mom must have had a rough time: carrying water in, washing clothes, taking care of four boys, cooking and catering to my dad's needs.

Old Maytag washer similar to the one our family owned

When I was born in 1954, my parents added two more rooms to the house. There were now two bedrooms, a kitchen and a living room. There was a double-size bed next to one wall for my two youngest brothers, and a single bed next to two other walls for my oldest brother and myself. Four boys in one small room was a tight fit! Every room in the house was painted a different color. The kitchen was a bright yellow, the bedrooms light green and blue, and the living room was a pale maroon color. The house wasn't insulated and had single pane windows. I remember in the wintertime how cold air would come in through cracks around the window sill. To keep warm we had so many quilts on the bed that you could barely turn over! Sometimes it got so cold in the house you could see your breath!

Sometime in the early 1960s water was piped in, but just to the sink. We still had the old Maytag wringer-type washer, and I remember that before water was piped into the house, I'd run a hose from the outside well to the washer and fill it up so it would be easier for Mom to do laundry. When the laundry was finished washing, I'd hook the hose to the drain pipe and run the wash water out into the yard. Then we'd fill the washer up again for the rinse. We didn't have a dryer of course, so the clothes were hung on a clothes line outside. In the summer this was okay, but sometimes in the winter the clothes would freeze. Then we'd have to bring everything inside and find a place to hang the clothes by the wood heater so they would eventually thaw out and dry. A pair of frozen jeans, if positioned exactly right, would stand on its own!

I don't remember where we got our clothes when we were small kids, but since we didn't have money to buy them, I think they were donated items from our church or other family members. We were poor farm kids, but not victims of multi-dimensional poverty; however, I do believe that my mom's and grandparents' generation would easily fall into that category. I remember going to first grade wearing a very worn flannel shirt, jeans, shoes, and a belt that were all too big for me! They called the clothes we wore *hand-me-downs*. There's a picture within this book of me wearing those clothes, and I don't think we could afford to go to a barber for haircuts at that time either because I had a very shaggy head of hair! After first grade, Mom decided to be the barber and gave us all a GI-style cut! I did not like it. Some of the kids at school teased us, and there were days that I did not want to go to school.

When we were growing up we didn't have a phone in the house; it wasn't until I had graduated from high school in 1972 that a phone was installed. Prior to that, we walked to Grandma's house and used her phone. She had a *party line*. There were four to six people on the same line. We would sometimes have to ask a stranger on the line if we could use the phone, especially if it was urgent. Some people would oblige, others would ignore us until they finished their conversation. A lot of the time the conversation was complete gossip!

Our bathroom was a *Johnny House*, basically a small building outside that sat over a deep hole in the ground. There was a wooden box type bench inside with a hole cut in it so when you did your business, it would go into the ground. Not very luxurious, but it met the need. I can remember having to go in the middle of the night, trudging through rain, wind, and snow sometimes knee deep.

We had no boots; we couldn't afford them, so we put plastic bread bags over our shoes and tied them at our ankles. This didn't work very well. The bags were slick and we'd fall down a lot! Water would eventually make its way inside, and we ended up with wet feet anyway! We'd have to go inside, take our shoes off and hang the socks up by the wood heater to dry. After our feet thawed out and the socks dried, we'd put more bags over our shoes and go right back out in the snow, either playing or bringing wood in for the fire. We wore out a lot of those bags in the wintertime! Eventually we were able to purchase some cheap goloshes that slipped over our shoes.

I remember one particular winter when we were all sick with the flu and didn't have any heat in the house. Some of us kids were literally shivering from the cold and from fevers. Dad's brother Owen came by to check on us, and when he saw that we had no heat, he went out and bought some coal, came back and started a fire in the little tin heater. All of us kids were huddled in a circle around that heater!

We spent the weekends at Grandma's house. That's where the extended family met, had Sunday dinner, and had actual face to face conversations. I like how communication was back then. We didn't see extended family members sometimes for weeks, so when they came to Grandma's, there was always a lot of catching up to do. One difference between then and now is that most family members just showed up unannounced for a visit. Most people were fine with that because we were glad to see our relatives. Fortunately, texting was not in existence back then, and we wouldn't have had time to do that anyway!

Of course we had many chores during the week: planting and harvesting our garden; shelling peas and butterbeans on Grandma's front porch, or in the backyard, under towering oak trees; working in the tobacco field and in the pack house, getting cured tobacco ready for the market in summer; raking leaves and mounds of acorns in the fall; cutting wood for heat in the winter; walking to the country store and bringing groceries and supplies home.

Some of my fondest recollections are of spending time with my brothers, Mom, Grandma, Grandpa and all the relatives that usually came to visit on Sundays. Dad stayed home since he preferred smaller groups. Grandma usually fixed a nice dinner (we called the noon meal *dinner*) consisting mostly of fresh vegetables and chicken cooked on the wood stove, and homemade bread baked in the oven. The aroma flooded the entire house!

Family gathering on Grandma's front porch (1969). Left to right: Joyce Keaton, Mabel Keaton, Bob O'Donnell, Mom, Ernest Keaton, and my grandparents D.L. and Maryland K. Newton in the glider

The front porch was where everyone gathered. Sometimes there were multiple conversations going on at one time. Sometimes there were serious conversations, other times just plain gossip. There was a swing on one end of the porch. When the swing went backwards, you floated out over part of the yard at the end of the porch. I was always afraid that the connection would come out of the ceiling and we'd land on the ground, but I'm glad to say that it never did! From the front porch, we could see cars going by on the two-lane road in front of Grandma's house. I dare say that being from a small community, we probably knew most of the people who passed by, especially if one of them honked the horn! The porch was a comforting and inviting place, especially when family you hadn't seen for a long time was there.

Mom's sister Thelma came from Richmond about every two weeks, and would spend the weekend. Mom's brother Crawley and his family, and Mom's younger sister Laura came every Sunday. We ate dinner, sat on the porch, took pictures and had a grand old time catching up on what everyone had been doing. We also enjoyed discussing our plans for the future. During this time together I don't think there were any problems in the world that we couldn't have solved on that porch!

In the summertime we'd make homemade ice cream on the front porch. Grandma had an old hand-crank ice cream maker which consisted of a wooden bucket with a canister in the middle. A crank handle was attached to the canister. She'd fill the canister with milk and sugar, adding diced peaches from her tree. Then she'd put ice and salt around the canister, and us kids would take turns rotating the crank until the mixture thickened. It was delicious!

There was one particular occasion that stands out in my mind. It was 1969 and Mom's cousin, Joyce Keaton, her husband, Bob O'Donnell, and Joyce's mother, Mabel, came from Wisconsin to visit. Ernest Keaton, my grandmother's brother, and Mabel met at some point when Ernest was working for the railroad and had traveled through the Milwaukee area. After a brief courtship, they were married and she moved to Mecklenburg County, Virginia with her new husband. When she arrived, she immediately went to work cooking, cleaning the house, working in the tobacco fields, and later, caring for their children. From what I hear from family, my great uncle Ernest wasn't the easiest person to get along with. Mabel Keaton left her husband Ernest when their children were pre-teens, and moved back to Wisconsin with the children. I don't know all the circumstances, but what is important to me is that we had multi-generations represented that day. It's something you don't see very often anymore, and I captured the event with an old Polaroid Swinger B&W camera.

I miss that togetherness of family. For the most part, people nowadays don't know who their extended family are, and don't take the time to find out. When older generations of my family were living there was a central place for people to meet, usually at my grandparents' house. Not only do we not see each other, traditions don't get shared and practiced, and genealogy information becomes vague or lost entirely. The last time I visited, I went to my grandmother's house and asked the lady who rents it now if I could go sit on the porch a few minutes. She obliged. A flood of memories washed through my mind, but it was eerily silent.

Southern Accents

In my hometown everyone had a distinct Southern Virgina accent. When we greeted a group of people we'd say "Hey, how y'all doin?" When greeting a single person, we'd say, "Hey, how ya doin?" Words like time, dime, prime, fine would be pronounced with a very flat *I*. A lot of the time we would misuse the words *sit* and *set*. For example, someone might say, "Just set yourself down in that chair." *Yeah* and *naw* were used for *yes* and *no*.

The words lay and lie were not used correctly, such as, "just lay down here and rest a spell." However, I think all the missteps in pronunciation lent itself to the warmth and charm that the area is known for. No, we weren't polished but we expressed a genuine desire to show our friendliness. The people who were born there have basically kept the same accent, but the area has seen more people move in, especially from the Northeast, who have entirely different accents. When I first came to California in 1990, people laughed at me when they heard me talk. They thought my expressions were weird. I ended up refining my speech to a certain degree in order to avoid so many comments. Sometimes I'd forget to switch back to my old way of talking when I visited family, and everyone would comment that I talked funny! So, when I visit family, I find myself switching back to my old way of talking. It sort of comes automatically once you're in a conversation.

Good Neighbors, Odd Jobs, and Photography

When my grandparents first bought their seventy-acre farm in 1947, neighbors helped each other. Neighbors nowadays mostly stay to themselves and don't want to be bothered. My grandmother related to me how the neighbors helped them cut trees off the property. They used mules to pull the logs to the area where their house and tobacco barns would eventually be built. Some of the logs were sent to a local saw mill in order to cut lumber for the house.

My grandpa's tobacco barns were constructed of rough logs, notched on the ends and stacked on top of each other. The barns were about twenty-five feet wide and approximately sixteen to twenty-four feet high. There were four to six tiers inside the barn, spaced four to five feet apart, so the sticks that held the tobacco could be hung in the barn. Grandpa's barn had four *rooms*, or sections of tier poles, with logs that had been hewn down much smaller than the structural logs. These smooth logs ran lengthwise starting at about six feet off the ground and going all the way to the top of the barn. Usually, we had two people inside the barn that straddled the tier poles and hung the sticks of tobacco from top to bottom. Neighbors also helped construct the tobacco packing house where tobacco was stored until it could be packed onto flat baskets or onto burlap bags, and then sent to the tobacco warehouse and sold to the tobacco companies at auction. There are no longer public auctions as there once were.

Tobacco is no longer cured in the old log barns. The old method was to burn wood in a fire box for a source of heat, or flue cured (heat transferred from large pipes inside the log barn). For a time, there were kerosene oil burners, then gas-fired burners used in log barns. Next came bulk barns, where the green tobacco was placed in racks in a metal box, heated with a forced-air gas burner. The advantage of bulk barns was to be able to cure loose leaf tobacco in bulk, without the added labor involved in manually tying tobacco on sticks and hanging it in the log barn. Nowadays, very large tobacco farms use highly mechanized harvesting equipment, and cure tobacco in what are called *box barns*. These barns enable farmers to cure very large quantities of green tobacco at a time and use the latest heated forced-air technologies. The tobacco is then *baled* like a bale of hay and sold under contract to the tobacco companies.

From my conversations with my grandmother, whenever a person in the community was ill or injured, neighbors came and helped keep the farm running. Farming communities were tight knit, and neighbors depended upon each other. As each generation has come and gone, farming and the camaraderie among neighbors has dwindled. In some more urban areas, it's a thing of the past. Being a good neighbor has changed. In the advent of a more service-oriented economy people often don't have time to be neighborly anymore. High-pressure jobs, a family, and an abundance of activities keep people focused on their own immediate sphere. It's sad that in some areas of the country being a good neighbor has come to mean keeping to oneself. I'm glad to hear that where I was raised, the good neighbor spirit is still functioning to some degree!

Us kids used to ride our bikes to see our friends, sometimes up to five miles away. Our parents gave us permission. It was different back then; people were more trustworthy. Parents weren't so worried about their kids being away from home because crime wasn't an issue like it is now. Living in the country at that time, we were far removed from that sort of thing. We never locked our doors at night and we never thought about intruders breaking in. Nowadays, unfortunately, drug dealing is prevalent in many rural areas of the country, including where I was raised, so one can't be too cautious.

We did work on the side, things like mowing grass, picking up bottles that people tossed out of their car windows, and picking wild blackberries to sell door to door for fifty cents a quart. I can remember when Grandpa Newton and I drove around with a lawnmower in his 1951 Ford truck and asked people if they needed their yards mowed. I was about twelve years old at the time. At the same time we asked if they needed their trash taken away. There was no residential trash collection in the county, and it remains the same today. Residents have to take their own trash to collection areas located in each community.

When I was thirteen, I took a Sunday job with a neighbor, delivering the *Greensboro Daily News*. I would have to get up at 5:00 a.m. and be ready to go when the neighbor came to pick me up. We drove about forty miles to Danville, VA to pick up the newspapers. On the drive back to South Boston, I would roll up the papers and put a rubber band around each one. There were about seventy-five subscribers in our area. I remember one Sunday it was raining and I slipped and fell, tore my pants and scraped my knee, but I kept on delivering the paper. When we finished our deliveries, we stopped at one of the family-owned restaurants in town and had breakfast.

I was sixteen when I got my driver's license. I remember having to parallel park on the street in front of the Division of Motor Vehicles. There were two yellow sticks laid out on the pavement and I had to park between them. I could barely see where they were! I didn't have a car, so I asked a neighbor if he'd take me to the DMV and let me use his car. He drove a big 1960s Ford Galaxy 500. It was in the middle of the summer, no air-conditioning in the car, and sweat was running down my back, and down the instructor's face. I guess he got tired of me running over the sticks, so he told me that I passed the test, I'm sure just to get out of the heat!

When I got my driver's license, the same neighbor who had the newspaper route, asked me to drive a big truck full of novelties, and help deliver the merchandise to local stores. I had not been driving but a couple of months and had to learn how to drive a vehicle that looked like a potato chip truck with a stick shift on the floor. During my first attempt at driving this humongous truck, I scraped the bumper on a car that was parked in front of us. It was a very old car and the owner didn't wish to deal with insurance. It was very scary, but I eventually got the hang of driving that truck! We used the extra money doing odd jobs to buy clothes for school, but for me, some of my extra money was put into a savings account, and some went towards buying film for my Kodak and Polaroid Swinger cameras.

I must have taken close to a thousand family pictures when I was a pre-teen and teenager. The photos I took are mostly the only record of my family: my brothers, mom, dad, aunts, uncles and cousins. I'd like to put them all in a giant printed book, but it seems like a daunting task. One picture in particular stands out. It's a picture of Mom and Dad, myself, and my three siblings. It was taken at the Hyco Road Ruitan Club in 2000, on the occasion of my parents' 50th wedding anniversary. There is no other existing picture with all of us in it. I was already living in California at the time, and had sent out invitations to our friends and family, had a wedding cake made, and was able to keep the entire event secret until Mom and Dad arrived. My partner, Brian, made a 3-D anniversary quilt in the shape of a bookcase. It has framed pictures of the family, books and a clock sitting on the shelves. It was the hit of the party!

Left to right: Douglas, Carl, Dad, Richard, Mom and David
at our parents' 50th wedding anniversary in 2000

I loved photography. It's a shame that I didn't make that my career. It's one of the things I had fun doing. I rarely turned the camera on myself though. Now I wish that I had, and that I had taken photos of us working in tobacco. I also love music but have never learned to play an instrument, except a small chord organ that I received for Christmas one year. I was told a long time ago that I was good at singing, and in the 70s and 80s I was part of a quartet that sang at churches and other functions. My advice: If you find something you're good at and enjoy, make it happen early on in your life.

Defining Events

All of us have defining events in our lives, things that mold us, mark a turning point in the direction our lives take, and contribute to us being who we are. There are events that are common to us all, such as: marriage, divorce, the birth of a child, the death of a loved one – all great life-changing events. Then there are more unique, individual moments and experiences that push us to become who we are. For me, there are several things that shaped my life the most: working in tobacco and textiles, a desire to obtain an education and to travel, and the work ethic my parents instilled in my brothers and myself.

Everyone has a story, myself included. Most people have a history too, usually filled with a lot of teachable moments. I was the second child born in the mid-1950s to poor farmers and mill workers. In my community, hardship was shared by just about everyone I knew. Everyone farmed tobacco in our community and throughout the county. Most of the farmers also worked in the local textile mill. I was no exception. In the busy world we lived in, it was scary to let go of the person I was many years ago, walking down a monotonous, barren, and endless road that branched off, seemingly into dead ends. Although I didn't like the direction my life was taking many years ago, a part of me, all these years later, still yearns to hear the freight trains rumbling in the distance, the rattle of our old window fan, the loud cracking of thunderstorms on a hot and humid night, my oldest brother's snoring, the lonesome call of the whippoorwills, the sounds of crickets that filled the night air, and the sounds of cicadas, only heard once every thirteen years.

As I write, it's May 2024 and the cicadas have emerged from the ground in my hometown. According to my brother, there were literally thousands of them clinging to the branches of maple trees at my parents' house, and the ground was covered in spots with their exoskeletons. What an extraordinary occurrence! All species have their own unique way of self-perpetuation.

In my mind I can still feel the stifling heat of an August day; no breeze, sweat dripping off my face, and so hot it can make you nauseous working in the tobacco fields. I can feel the numbing cold of a harsh, howling winter wind, blowing out of the north, as I split wood for the wood heater in our tiny, crowded kitchen. I can feel the cool, refreshing water of the creek my friends and I played in as kids, sailing through the air and creating a giant splash amid screams of delight for relief from the heat. I can smell the aroma of fresh bread baking in the oven of my grandmother's wood cook stove. Life was often hard, but the things life showed me will be a part of who I am forever. The photographic images of my early life are all black and white, yet my memories of that time are all in full color, as vivid as the roses and irises that Mom grew.

In my mind I can see Mom and Grandma making quilts in Grandma's living room, and I can hear the laughter of family gathered together at Christmas. I can see buckets of peas and butterbeans that we shelled until our fingers were sore and stained purple while sitting on the front porch catching up on everyone's lives. And I can feel the late summer breeze and hear the conversations as I reminisce with Mom, Grandmother and other relatives under the towering oak trees of her back yard. Their voices have all floated away on that breeze, yet I can still recall them. It is comforting.

Farm Life

Although my brother has remodeled our childhood home, the surrounding area seems somewhat ghostly now. There are only a few phantom reminders of the endless toil that was part of being a farmer in the South: a broken plow handle protruding from a thicket that once was a field of tobacco, a broken-down wooden trailer sitting under a swaying hull of a storage shed, an old log barn crumbling with decay from forty years of unuse.

Long ago the barn held tobacco, fresh from the fields for curing, and there was a tobacco pack house that once held cured tobacco. The pack house is now gradually sinking into the ground. Behind the pack house was a stall where the mule was kept and fed. Years later, we used the space to store potatoes in a bed of straw to protect them from the ravages of a cold and unforgiving winter. Old buildings, seemingly still held together only by memories.

According to my brother, the second story of the pack house is fast approaching ground level! The many years of rain washing down the hill behind my parents' house, soaking underneath the foundation, sometimes in torrents from thunderstorms, has taken its toll on that beautiful, old log building that was a testament to the ingenuity of a hard-working farmer.

With their bare hands, with much sweat and determination, my grandparents, D.L. and Maryland Keaton Newton, built three tobacco barns and a pack house for storing cured tobacco until it was ready to be taken to the tobacco warehouse market. The fields that grew tobacco are now all covered in trees once again, as they were when my grandparents first bought the farm. Nature has renewed itself. It has come full circle. Hard work is all my parents and grandparents knew, and they made sure that their work ethic was emblazoned into the minds of their children from an early age!

My maternal grandparents were share-croppers when Herbert Hoover was President. They moved from farm to farm, working in tobacco fields for fifty cents a day. Not much money by twenty-first century standards, but they survived because their will to survive was strong. Those kinds of wages were only meant for survival. My Grandma Newton was smart when it came to business. She found odd jobs to make extra money, such as doing other people's laundry, picking and selling wild blackberries, selling eggs and chickens that she raised. Sometimes she grew extra vegetables and sold those as well. Somehow, Grandma managed to save enough money to buy a seventy-acre farm which had a government tobacco allotment on it, seven acres as I recall. If she didn't have enough money, I'm sure she borrowed some from the original landowner.

My grandparents began to clear land, cutting trees with a cross-cut saw. They had one mule which they harnessed with ropes and chains to pull up the tree stumps. After much labor the land was cleared, plowed and made ready to plant. My mom related to me how she physically dug up tree roots out of the soil until her hands were blistered. The land that they cleared was referred to as the *new ground*. This was land that had never been farmed before. Even when we stopped farming, the land was still referred to as the new ground. The land provided a chance for a new beginning, and a legacy for their children and grandchildren.

Self-sufficiency was all that they knew. Nothing was ever handed to them; they worked for everything they got.

Not only did they clear the land, they used the trees to construct their home, three tobacco curing barns and a packing house. At this writing, the last tobacco barn they built is still standing. The last crop went into that barn around 1975. The pack house building has almost completely collapsed. Tobacco was the main cash crop in Virginia and had been for hundreds of years. Raising a crop of tobacco was intensely laborious.

Tobacco Was King

Tobacco farming was common in the countryside of Southern Virginia. As far back as I can remember, which would be when I was ten or eleven years old (1964), we worked a tobacco crop. At that time, children of farmers were expected to work, maybe not as hard as the adults, but us kids were each assigned tasks to complete. No matter what the job was, we were expected to do that job. Every job, no matter how great or small, contributed towards the completion of a larger task.

We had three different areas where we had tobacco crops, two fields on my grandmother's farm, and one about a mile from our house on a neighbor's farm. The total combined acreage we farmed was about seven acres. The fields on my grandmother's property were accessible by a one-lane dirt road. To get to one particular field, we had to drive a tractor with a big wooden trailer attached to it about a mile down a winding dirt road This road was very steep in places, with areas that had washed out during the many thunderstorms we had in the summer. The road crosses the creek where us kids played in occasionally.

Along this creek bed is where my oldest brother attempted to grow marijuana at one time. Mom and Grandma found the marijuana patch and dug up every plant! Strangely enough, my brother never asked any questions, although he did get into trouble over this. Apparently, he was selling or helping someone sell marijuana and got locked up. Mom talked to a friend who was a member of the Halifax County Board of Supervisors, and he was able to assist in getting probation for my brother. At that time, he could have gone to prison for a long time!

Planting On The Owen Howerton Farm

Photo that appeared in the local newspaper, Gazette Virginian

Getting back to the crops: One brother drove the tractor while Mom, my other brothers and myself rode the rickety old wooden trailer, along with whatever supplies we needed for the field work. We took a two-gallon glass jar full of water and ice cubes because usually the weather was hot and humid, and it was too far to go back to the house if we needed more to drink. Each of us would take turns drinking from the jar. We usually planted a few tomato plants at the end of a tobacco row, so we'd have a snack to eat if we got hungry. On one of our trips to the field past the creek, Mom got sick. It had been very hot that day and she was working in the sun and not drinking much water. When we got home, I convinced her to see a doctor. The doctor said that Mom had gotten very dehydrated and was close to having a heat stroke. After resting and drinking fluids, she was okay. Laboring in the heat was just one of the negative aspects of working in tobacco.

Traveling back and forth to work in the fields gave me a lot of time to ponder my situation. Would I be doing this for a long time, or was there something else in the cards for me at the end of that dirt road. Or maybe my life would take another direction down some other road? At the time, I felt alone and helpless to change my situation.

A tobacco crop began by creating a *plant bed*, clearing a spot of land close to the house to start the plants from seed. Depending on how many acres of tobacco we were planting, there could be multiple plant beds, each measuring about twenty feet wide by forty feet long. A cheesecloth-like cover was placed over the beds, attached to poles along the edges. The cover was used to protect the plants from early frosts, which were notoriously unpredictable in Southern Virginia. Before the tobacco seeds were sown in the plant beds, I remember from experience, that farmers were using a substance in a can, called Methyl Bromide, which was a gas used to control fungi, weeds, insects and nematodes in the soil. At the time, in the mid-1960s, this gas came in canisters which were stuck into the ground inside the plastic-covered plant beds and punctured to release the gas into the soil. We didn't know it at the time, but Methyl Bromide was very toxic and could have caused damage to the lungs, eyes and skin if exposed to it. Thankfully, alternatives to this type of fumigant exist today.

When the plants sprouted and grew about hand high, we sprinkled a dust called Fermate on the young plants to prevent a disease called Blue Mold. Fermate was another toxic substance, that if breathed could cause respiratory issues. We did not know what physical issues would result from handling plants without gloves or breathing toxic dust. We then pulled the plants individually, loaded them in boxes and took them to whatever field we were working in. This was the point at which the tobacco plants were *transplanted*, or moved from their birth place to their new home. The land of course would previously have been tilled, fertilized, and rows laid out by a tractor, or in earlier times, by a mule and plow.

A barrel was attached to the tractor for carrying water for the plants. We had a mechanical tobacco planter attached to the back of the tractor. It had two seats for those of us who handled the plants, and a bin in front of us which held the plants. To get the plant into the ground, an arm with a clamp would rotate around as the tractor moved along. An attachment near the rows would open the row. Working with Mom, my job would be to place a tobacco plant in the clamp as the arm rotated around. The plant would go down into the soil and a small amount of water would flow from the barrel.

We could only plant one row at a time, and those rows seemed to just get longer as the day passed. My uncle actually had a field of tobacco with rows so long that you could not see the end. Click clack, click clack, was the sound we heard for hours; we only stopped to load more plants and water, or to sip some water to quench our thirst. The monotony was excruciating! One of my brothers would walk behind the planter with a small wooden peg and a handful of plants to fill in spots that we missed. In the old days, entire fields were planted using that wooden peg. The peg eventually gave rise to a hand planter contraption. It was made of metal and was very heavy and cumbersome. One of us had to continually supply plants and water for this process to be productive.

Once plants were established, we were at the mercy of the weather. If it rained, everything was okay. If not, then we had to consider irrigation, if there was a water source nearby. Most, but not all, tobacco crops were planted near a water source. I remember quite vividly a time when there had not been any rain for an extended period. The plants that were already in the field were suffering in a drought. There was a small pond where us kids and our best friends often fished, so we got permission from the owner to use some of the water. My dad had a friend who had irrigation pipes, so us kids who were old enough, in addition to some hired help, laid aluminum pipes from the pond to the tobacco field. The distance between the pond and the field was about a quarter of a mile. After the pipes were laid, sprinklers had to be attached intermittently along the pipes. Once everything was all in place, my dad attached a pump to his Ferguson tractor and started the engine. Water began to flow from the pond to the field. We couldn't use a lot, because the pond level would go too low. At the time I thought it was an exercise in futility, but the crop survived and not too much time passed before we had rain again.

In addition to the hot dry summers, sometimes there would be too much rain, and some of the plants would drown. At that point we'd have to trudge through the mud and dig drainage ditches at the ends of rows to let the excess water out, and sometimes replant large sections of a field by hand. If this happened, we would have to go in later with a garden hoe and dig the grass out until things dried out enough to get the tractor in the field. Then there was always the chance that hail from a thunderstorm would destroy the entire crop, or wind would blow the plants over, resulting in us having to set the plants up again by pressing dirt around the plants with our feet. Most farmers had hail/crop insurance, which added more to the cost of raising a crop.

When the tobacco was a little more than hand high, Dad would till along the sides of the rows to mitigate the growth of weeds. Us kids and Mom followed behind the tractor with a garden hoe, weeding in between the plants and uncovering some of the leaves that were buried by the tractor cultivators. When my brothers Carl and David were old enough to drive the tractor, they spent many hours each week cultivating the crop. Eventually the plants were too big for a tractor to go over them, and cultivating was no longer necessary.

Then there were chemicals, dust in particular, that had to be applied to each plant to keep the bugs and tobacco worms from eating the plants. I remember my brothers and I would cut up an old burlap bag into small pieces, big enough to hold what was called Sevin Dust, a pesticide that people used regularly on their garden plants to control insects. If there was a breeze while we were dusting tobacco, we would breathe in the dust. No masks were worn. At the time, we didn't realize all the hidden dangers of using pesticides.

At times when we could afford it, Dad would hire a crop duster to fly over the fields and spray poison on the plants. Of course, us kids were thrilled to watch an airplane zooming over the field. I have no doubt that we inhaled both the dust we used and the spray that the airplane deposited, not to mention the runoff that went into the nearby creek whenever it rained. My brother Carl related to me that we were actually working in a field one time when the plane was spraying. We ran out of the field but later returned to work, as the poison dripped off the tobacco. We all were sickened as a result of this event.

After watching the airplane fly over the fields, us kids and our friends would pretend we were airplanes and zoom through the field, breaking leaves off the tobacco plants as we went along. That particular incident did not go unnoticed by my grandpa. He confronted us and we told him what happened. When we got home, we got a *switch* to our legs resulting in red whelps! Our twin friends had to go and apologize to my grandpa, and pull their pants down to show him the red marks on their butts left by their dad! Needless to say, we learned our lesson!

Tobacco field (photo courtesy of Billy Wagner 2023)

When the tobacco was four or five feet tall, it began to produce seed flowers in the top. It was during the hot muggy days of July that we then had to go plant by plant, breaking out all the flowers until we had blisters on our hands. By doing this, the growth was redirected into the leaves. A farmer wanted weight in the leaves, because this would mean more money at the time the crop was cured and sold at market.

Breaking out the flowers caused secondary growths called *suckers* to appear between the leaves. Guess what, now we had to go over the entire crop and pull the suckers out, otherwise they would take over the entire crop and prevent weight from going into the leaves. Those growths, if left unchecked, would end up being almost as big as the tobacco plant. In the late 1960s and early 1970s, chemicals became available that could be poured onto the plant from a bottle by hand that prevented the growths from occurring. I remember routinely getting my hands wet with the poison, which was called *Off-Shoot-T*.

I remember getting contact dermatitis and being physically sick from handling chemicals without gloves or masks. I visited our family doctor a few times for this issue, and he suggested that I stop my exposure to the chemicals, and even to stop handling green and cured tobacco. Of course, I could not do that because we were expected to help with the crop. However, we could have used gloves and a mask, had we realized the harmful effects of the various poisons that were used on tobacco. I learned later that the Nicotine in green and dried tobacco is extremely toxic. Somehow, we didn't know that we should be wearing protection when using poisonous chemicals. To this day, I still have contact dermatitis on my fingertips and have to use a medication on them from time to time.

At some point later on, my dad bought a sprayer system that attached to the tractor. Up and down the rows he'd go, spraying poison on the plants for suckers and insect control. I'm sure whenever the wind was blowing, he inhaled it. In every phase of tobacco farming, we used chemicals, pesticides and fumigants. I remember being nauseous from smelling the green tobacco out in the hot sun, and from mixing the various concoctions to control one pest or another.

Now that I look back on my days working in tobacco, we were trying to grow the perfect plant, but didn't realize that handling tobacco and the chemicals used in tobacco production, could have been hazardous to our health, and that smoking tobacco could cause serious illnesses and death in some instances. We were poor and the crop meant that we could afford things that we wouldn't ordinarily have. Being able to provide a better living for your family took precedence over many other issues, sometimes including health. Thankfully, safer methods of pest control are currently being used.

The things I remember most about working in tobacco are being out in the suffocating heat and humidity, being hot and dirty, and not being able to play very much with our friends. And there were many times as I sat on that rickety old wooden trailer, bouncing up and down, heading to work in a field, that I thought, "I will never escape this torture!" I felt disconnected from the rest of the world. At the same time, I realized that tobacco farming was providing our family with needed income. Nowadays, if we did not have farmers growing vegetables and fruit, the world would starve! I have immense respect for farmers but working in tobacco wasn't what I wanted to do. Of course, now that I'm older, there is a certain nostalgia about being in a simpler time and place, and even though at times I felt hopeless, those experiences grounded me and taught me the importance of a person making their own way in the world.

When I was a child, entire families depended on tobacco for their livelihood. There were many small farmers trying to eke out a living from the rich soil of Southern Virginia. Money crops that could provide the bulk of a family's income were very limited. Corn was grown more for animal feed than for cash. Soybeans and peanuts could provide only a small return on investment. There were also fields of golden wheat growing all around, but this was primarily used to make flour at the local mill (Keystone Mills). Of course, this flour was used by local families to make bread. I remember as a young child, seeing the combine slowly making its way down the two-lane country road that we lived on. I don't remember where it originated, only that it traveled from farm to farm, harvesting wheat in late summer. Us kids would usually run along beside it, and if we found out where it was headed, we'd follow along and watch it thrash a field of wheat. This was exciting stuff for a young kid living in a rural area with limited access to entertainment!

Tobacco would yield more earnings per acre than all other crops combined, but it was a very labor-intensive crop. There was a lot of poor labor waiting around, and farms didn't have strict child labor laws at the time. My recollection of working in tobacco harvesting started around the time I was ten years old, in 1964. Harvesting began around the middle of July and usually finished in early September before school started. I recall that there were times when the tobacco crop was late being planted due to the fields being too wet to work or temperatures being too cold. This resulted in the harvest coming later in the fall. In those instances, school was sometimes delayed for a couple of weeks so harvesting could be finished.

Tobacco was harvested by hand. A stalk of tobacco would have twenty or more large leaves which matured at different times. We would pick off two to three leaves each week for about six weeks in the summer. Usually around four men and/or boys were needed in the field, and about six women and children worked at the barns. I remember my dad driving around to different farms in the community, trying to line up help for the work the next day. We had no phone until after I graduated from high school, so contacting people happened in person. I'm talking children ten or eleven years old. Children living on a farm at that time were much more mature at that age than they are nowadays.

They had to be. There was no other choice but to work. There were no soccer games, no piano lessons, no video games, no cell phones and no hanging out with your friends, unless the work had been finished. I'm sure some may find it shocking to think that children were being reared in such a primitive and harsh environment!

Work began between 6:00 and 7:00 a.m. Quite often we would have to empty a barn of cured tobacco the same morning that we intended to fill it with newly harvested tobacco. Four young men called *croppers* or *pullers* would each take a row of tobacco and break off the leaves and put them in slides or carts. One or two people would drive the mules (or tractors if you had them), and pull the slides or carts to and from the fields, delivering the picked tobacco to the barn. Slides were wooden frames, enclosed on the bottom with runners, which made them easier to move. The sides were lined with burlap bags to hold the tobacco leaves inside. We'd unhook the full container and hook up an empty one, and back to the field my dad would go for another load. Workers would remain in the field, picking the leaves while my dad went to the barn.

Once at the barn, there were women and children who moved the tobacco from the slides to a bench, which was under a shed that was attached to the barn. There were usually two women called *stringers*, and two children called *handers* for each stringer. The handers picked up three to four tobacco leaves in a bundle and handed them to the stringers, who looped tobacco twine around the stems and wove the bundles onto wooden tobacco sticks. The sticks were rough-hewn pieces of wood about four feet long, and about an inch and a half around. They would be stored and reused each time a barn was filled. Once a stringer completed filling a tobacco stick, a designated person laid the stick on the ground, forming a long stack as things progressed.

Sometime before 10:00 a.m. one of the barn workers would go around and make a list of food for break time and dinner (lunch). We bought snacks from the local country store. There were items such as Vienna sausage, pork & beans, potted meat, peanut butter crackers, honey buns, moon pies and regular saltines. Not exactly a gourmet meal! To drink, we'd get Pepsi's, Coke's and RC Cola's. First break was usually around 10:00 a.m., and then dinner around noon, or as soon as the last leaves were tied.

From my recollection of our farm work, once the croppers or pullers finished picking over the fields, they returned to the barn and started hanging all those accumulated sticks of tied tobacco inside a barn for curing. When we took our breaks, we would have conversations about whatever was going on in the community. We would call this *social media* nowadays! The only device we had was word of mouth. We'd talk about things like who got married, what happened at church, the work we had to do when we finished with the tobacco, and how school was going. Everything we planned back then was centered around the crop. Everything else pretty much took a back seat.

I was ten years old when I started working in tobacco, two to four days a week, four to six hours a day, five days a week in the summer. As I mentioned earlier, we started work between 6:00 and 7:00 a.m. I started at the barn as a hander, and at thirteen graduated to pulling the leaves in the fields, out in the hot sun, or sometimes in the cold rain. I remember times when we still had tobacco in the fields in early October. There would be a very heavy and cold dew on the plants and we were soaking wet and freezing by the time we finished and got back to the barn! Then there were other times during the summer when we'd get unexpected thunderstorms. Water would drip down on us when we hung the sticks of wet tobacco inside the barn! When I was seventeen, I was working five days a week, five to six hours a day. We usually tried to finish filling a barn by 11:00 a.m. or 12:00 noon. When we weren't working in our crop, we'd find neighbors who needed help and get paid for our work. Mom worked with us, and when everything was finished, she still had to get the noon meal prepared, and start doing laundry. More about Mom's hard work later.

Tobacco slides (or carts) used to bring green tobacco in from the field
(photo courtesy of Billy Wagner)

Tobacco was planted on raised rows for several reasons. The process of plowing the dirt between the rows to dig up weeds and grass created deep furrows. Having raised rows with deep furrows in between prevented the tobacco from drowning or falling over in heavy rains. We picked the leaves, starting at the bottom of the plant, so having raised rows also kept the bottom leaves out of the dirt and it wasn't quite so far to bend down to pick them. But having a lot of loose dirt piled up into rows created muddy conditions when it rained excessively. I would sometimes sink in the mud pass my ankles, and would even lose my shoes when I stepped on a row in wet weather. Some years it was so wet that the tractor would get stuck over and over. Sometimes, storm winds would blow the tobacco plants over and we'd have to spend a day trying to set plants up again. When we'd set up a plant, it would sometimes fall back down again. The same scenario happened with our corn crop.

There are more difficult crops to harvest than tobacco: picking strawberries, digging sweet potatoes, picking turnip greens, or any kind of labor requiring one to stoop or squat. All of them are backbreaking, but harvesting those crops only lasted a few weeks at most. Out of all the crops we planted, tobacco was the most labor-intensive. Harvesting usually started at the beginning of July, when the summer sun was the hottest. Pulling tobacco lasted for six or seven weeks, all through the sweltering days of July and into August. We walked for hours bent over. Try walking around the yard or house for an hour, touching your toes the whole time. Now imagine that for several hours in sweltering heat!

Tobacco has a heavy tar, especially on the bottom of the leaves. As I walked down a row picking leaves, sweat ran into my eyes when I bent over. In a very short time, my hands and forearms would begin to accumulate a coating of heavy, sticky, black tar that caused the leaves to pull at my arms with extra friction as I reached from plant to plant. I remember reaching down occasionally and grabbing a handful of dirt and plastering it on the tar to stop it from being so sticky. This resulted in layers of black tar as the day wore on, making you that much hotter. You could wear long sleeves to cut down on this problem, but then you were hot from wearing the long sleeves in 90-degree heat. By the end of the day, you were coated with tar and dirt and sweat, for about $5.00 to $10.00 a day (in the 1970s). And getting that tar off was difficult; soap didn't clean it very well. We used lye soap if we could get it. This was a homemade concoction that was made from lye and bacon grease, heated in a big black pot over a wood fire.

Green tobacco from the field was stacked on a long bench under a shed that was attached to the barn. Three leaves at a time were picked up off the bench and handed to a *stringer*, a person who'd tie the leaves onto a four-foot-long stick. However, the last couple of years that we farmed, we bought an electric stringer. It worked just like a sewing machine. We'd put a layer of tobacco leaves on the conveyor belt, lay a tobacco stick on the first layer, and put another layer of leaves on top of the stick. The conveyor belt would move along and a pre-threaded giant needle would pull twine from a large ball of twine sitting in a bucket on the ground, and sew the two layers of leaves onto the stick. It was more trouble than it was worth! The contraption would continuously break down, and leaves would fall off the stick, so that you had to pick them up and re-sew them over and over again! Nevertheless, we used this machine until we stopped farming around 1975.

After the tobacco had been harvested, tied onto sticks and laid onto the ground in a long stack, we passed each stick into the barn, like an assembly line process. There were long poles inside the barn called *tier poles* that went from one side to another. Each stick of tobacco was hung between two of these poles until the barn was filled up. There were usually about three or four hundred sticks of green tobacco in a barn.

In the old days when my grandparents farmed, they used wood to cure the tobacco. There were two fire boxes or furnaces on the outside of the barn. They were built from cinder blocks or stones, and extended a short distance into the barn. Large metal flue pipes were attached to the fire boxes and ran (raised) along the floor of the barn so heat could be distributed evenly. Vent pipes were located outside the barn to carry smoke and other gases out. This process of curing the green tobacco usually took about a week. Someone would have to stay at the barn 24/7 to keep the fire going. I remember going with my grandpa to the barn on at least one occasion and sleeping on a blanket on the ground.

Unfortunately, fire broke out in two of the barns and they burned to the ground. This was probably in the late 1940s or early 1950s. Remains of the foundations of these barns can still be seen on their property. Later on, in the 70s, gas burners took the place of wood flues, and nowadays the tobacco is cured in *bulk* or *box* barns, trailer-like buildings where the tobacco can just be dumped inside in no particular order, certainly not the order in which we had to endure in the 1960s.

One thing that I vividly remember about working in tobacco is getting up early in the morning, standing on the back porch, and taking in the aroma of freshly cured tobacco floating on the air from the barn, or having that same experience while working in the pack house, or hanging around at the warehouse, waiting for our check to be processed for the tobacco we had brought to market. It was undeniably a very intoxicating aroma. I remember wondering how something that smelled so good, and provided economic relief to so many, could be so harmful?

Child Labor and Health

M uch has been written about child labor laws, and the dangers associated with children working in tobacco. I had planned to publish excerpts from a couple of reputable organizations that follow child labor, especially when working on tobacco farms, but could not get permission, so I rely on my knowledge of working in tobacco and the experiences of family and friends.

When our family farmed tobacco, the health of myself, my siblings and parents was at risk. Not only was this true on tobacco farms, but in other farming operations as well. Unfortunately, U.S. laws do not offer the same protections for children working in agriculture as they do for children working in other areas of employment. Children aged twelve and thirteen can legally work unlimited hours on farms of any size, outside of school hours, with their parent's permission. While working in tobacco years ago, I witnessed children, myself included, who became ill from being exposed to green tobacco in the fields, and dried tobacco after curing. Over the years of working in tobacco I have seen and experienced the sudden onset of serious symptoms while working in tobacco fields or in the tobacco pack house: nausea, vomiting, loss of appetite, headaches, dizziness, skin rashes, difficulty breathing, irritation to the eyes.

I mentioned earlier in my writing that I still occasionally have contact dermatitis on my fingertips. When I first saw a doctor about this condition, he told me I would most likely continue to have it, and that it was a result of handling tobacco, and especially the chemicals used on tobacco plants. I have experienced many of the symptoms mentioned above, and knew other families who had children who experienced these symptoms as well.

I have discussed this with my youngest brother and he related to me how he was sickened by the use of chemicals, working in the hot tobacco field and in the pack house, handling cured tobacco. According to my doctor during visits as a teen, the symptoms mentioned above are consistent with acute nicotine poisoning. When I worked in the fields, or handled green or dried tobacco, I became ill. My doctor advised me not to work in tobacco, but at the time, this was how most people we knew made their living. If we got sick, it was just shrugged off, and after a while of non-exposure, things started to get better. But I remember being very ill, to the point of not eating after working in tobacco. I was also very underweight throughout my teen years.

I know this will rankle a lot of people's pride who worked in tobacco, and at the time, I felt the same pride. I built a huge work ethic by working on the farm, not to mention the financial sustenance provided by the work. To a certain degree, I still feel pride for what we accomplished, but the dangers involved are something that I experienced. If people are going to grow tobacco, they need to protect themselves from contact with the plants, and exposure to the chemicals. At the time, I'm sure we didn't think the illnesses were related to tobacco. I am not a medical expert; I write this from self-experience to provide information and awareness.

According to the *U.S. Department of Labor* website, children under age twelve can work on small farms, especially family farms with parental permission, and where employees are exempt from the federal minimum wage requirement. Children over the age of thirteen can work in any agricultural occupation during non-school hours, excluding those occupations considered hazardous. An example would be operating machinery such as a cotton or corn picker, or changing equipment for one purpose or another. There are numerous examples of hazardous jobs listed on the Department of Labor website. Minors who are at least sixteen years of age can perform any farm job, including agricultural occupations deemed hazardous by the Secretary of Labor, at any time, including during school hours.

In contrast U.S. child labor laws generally prohibit the employment of minors in *non-agricultural* occupations under the age of 14, restrict the hours and types of work that can be performed by minors under age sixteen, and prohibit the employment of minors under the age of 18 in any hazardous occupation.

Hyco Road Grocery (2024)

The Country Store

When my grandparents moved to their new farm in 1947, grocery stores were not prevalent in the rural South. Small, rural country stores were scattered throughout the countryside instead. They carried basic necessities: bread, sugar, hoop cheese, a few canned goods, coffee, gas for vehicles and kerosene for lamps. The country store was a meeting place for people, especially those older individuals who were retired, and a magical place for kids of all ages. I remember there was a pot-bellied coal-burning stove at the far end of the store in my community. People would sit around the stove in winter, discussing politics, the weather of course, and in summer, how the crops were doing. Some would talk about their jobs and families, their church services, and learn about who's new to the neighborhood. In those days we didn't watch much television. The news we got was mostly by word of mouth.

In the mid-to-late 1960s, my brothers and I and our friends would stop in to get soft drinks from the cold ice boxes, candy, and bubblegum that had baseball trading cards in the pack. The bubblegum wrappers had different comic strips printed on them. During that time, the soft drinks were in glass bottles with metal bottle caps. There was a time when the companies printed prize money inside the caps. I remember winning $10 in an RC Cola bottle cap when I was about twelve or thirteen years old. We all had a grand old time with that money!

We hardly missed a day stopping at the country store. In fact, there were three stores within a couple of miles of us, so when we went to softball games, there was a store within walking distance. If we went fishing at the pond, there was another store close by. They are all mostly gone now, and have been replaced by large supermarket and convenience store chains. However, our country store is still there, but is now used as a residence. Those little stores offered a quaint, laid back and carefree time in our lives.

One of my childhood friends related a story to me recently about the very first owner of our store, which was called Hyco Road Grocery (named after the country road we lived on). He said that the owner asked if he and his twin brother would rake up some acorns in the back yard and feed them to his pigs. Of course they obliged, thinking that they would get some money to spend in the store. After a few hours of work, they finished the job and informed the owner. He gave each of them two pieces of bubblegum! My friends were so angry, but they accepted the payment and never volunteered to do work for him again!

Our country store did not have an alcohol license when it first opened, so those customers who wanted to buy beer were permitted by one of the store owners to come to the back door at midnight and they could purchase it when the public wasn't around. This was illegal of course, but eventually the new owner obtained a license. Many of the farmers in the area, as well as my family, had an account at the country store, and purchased goods *on time*. Food for the farm help, gasoline for their equipment and other necessities were charged. Our family also bought a few basic staples there. My mom would make a list and send us to the store. We would walk there and carry the items back home. Those stores were a lifeline to the farming community.

The Garden, the Pig Pen and the Chicken Coop

As far back as when I was about ten years old, I remember my parents and grandparents planting huge gardens. They each had orchards of pears, peaches, apples and plums. They canned literally hundreds of jars of various produce, and made jams and preserves from the fruit.

This was our survival. We did not have a lot of money to spend at a store, so we raised most of our food. We had fields of corn, rows and rows of butter beans, purple hull peas, snap beans, potatoes, tomatoes, squash, turnip greens, cabbage and peppers. All of us kids had to help plant, weed and pick the garden. We all pitched in to shell the beans and peas and even peeled tomatoes for canning. Sometimes we hauled the produce next door to Grandma's house, sat on her big front porch, and shelled beans for hours! Somehow it seemed less of a chore when we did it at her house. Mom was in charge of the actual canning or freezing process. Mom had a homemade, stone barbecue outside where she boiled the jars of vegetables after canning. I would help her keep the fire going by making sure there was an ample supply of wood nearby.

Living on a farm, we raised pigs for meat, had a cow for milk, and chickens for meat and eggs. We had a pig pen with a trough for food and water, a pasture for the cow and a coop for the chickens. I remember my brothers and I pulling weeds and raking acorns to give to the young pigs. When pigs were more than three years old and weighed at least a hundred and twenty pounds they were considered hogs. We also gave them table scraps and locally bought feed. I remember my dad saying, "Ya'll get going and slop the hogs!" *Slopping* meant feeding the hogs. My parents and grandparents had chickens primarily to produce eggs, but occasionally one of the them ended up on the supper plate! Mom related to me that when she was a child, she had a chicken that she named *Speck*. Speck laid eggs, so she was able to live out her life on the farm. The one thing I wouldn't participate in was when it came time to slaughter the hogs. I could not bear to watch that. But it was survival, and at the time, it was what we knew had to be done if we were to survive.

The Barn and the Packhouse

It must have been an amazing feat to be able to construct log barns out of trees, cut from their own property, as my grandparents did. As many as 100 logs went into construction of a tobacco barn. At this writing, there is still one barn standing on the property. Sadly, it is in a state of disrepair, and unfortunately will not be standing many more years. I remember as a kid, we had to daub the cracks in between the logs in that barn every spring. We simply dug clay out of the ground, mixed it with water, and chinked it into the cracks between the logs. This was done so the building would be air tight, and not lose so much of the heat during the tobacco curing process. There is a lot of red clay in the land that my grandparents owned, just perfect for filling in the cracks!

On a visit there several years ago, I walked by the old barn, and the hole where we dug the clay is still there. It hasn't been filled in by nature. I've lived in California over thirty years now, but each time I go home I visit that old barn and snap a picture of it because one day it will no longer be there. My pictures will provide future family members with a record of how our lives used to be.

It's an eerie feeling to walk on the land that we once farmed, and it's hard to believe so much time has passed. Nature has reclaimed the land. Trees have regrown on the land that my grandparents cleared nearly eighty years ago. Wild blackberries have sprouted everywhere, another reminder of yet an additional task we did as kids: picking blackberries and selling them. As kids, my brothers, our friends and myself would put kerosene on our socks and pants, and around our ankles, before going out to pick those blackberries. If we didn't, we'd come home full of ticks and chiggers! We didn't have bug repellent back then, so we improvised!

Grandpa's old tobacco barn (built circa 1947)

There are so many reminders of what once was, and it's my history, a history that is important in defining who one is and where one comes from. Yet this one testament to our hard work, this old log building, still remains, and would have remained many years in the future had the new owners of my grandparents' property maintained it in a minimal state of repair.

Sometimes when I've visited the property, I've gotten the most vivid flashbacks of people talking about their families, desires and hardships while working. I can hear the tractor in the distance, straining as it makes its way to the barn with a slide full of fresh tobacco leaves. I can feel the hunger pangs begin to overwhelm me as I anticipate the noon-day meal. I can feel the intense heat of the mid-day sun, beating down on me, and can hear the distant clap of thunder, signaling an approaching storm.

I can see the faces of our friends and family, many of whom are no longer with us. I can hear their laughter and can see the serious concerns on their faces. When I'm there, I begin to think about the happy times, the sad times and the camaraderie we shared that gave us some sort of purpose to our lives as we toiled away, trying to eke out a living from the land, and not knowing from one day to the next if our labor would pay off. They are all motionless figures now, but time has marched forward.

Once the tobacco had cured, we hooked a big trailer to our tractor and drove it to the barn. We emptied the tobacco from the barn to the trailer and drove it to the other side of the property to a *pack house.* We also rented five acres on a friend's farm about two miles from my grandmother's farm, so we sometimes had to haul this humongous load of cured tobacco on the main road, with cars honking at us along the way. The pile of tobacco, and us, swayed back and forth on the trailer. We would cling desperately to the stack of tobacco, trying to keep ourselves and the tobacco from tumbling over! One bump in the road, or a sudden move at the wheel could have spelled disaster! We didn't dare try to move a load of cured tobacco on a windy day! We never lost a load though. Can you imagine picking up sticks of dried tobacco in the middle of the highway with cars zooming by?

Once we unloaded the trailer from Grandpa's barn, or the barn on the rented farm, we'd *strip* the tobacco off the sticks and stack it in the corner of the packhouse until we were ready to pack it on burlap bags. If the leaves were too dry, we had a spray tank that we filled with water and lightly sprayed the stacks of dried tobacco to get them *in order*, or supple enough to pack on the burlap sheets. We also had an underground *pit* where we'd hang tobacco for the same purpose. I did not like going into the pit. It was dark and scary, and snakes liked to hide out there!

Grandpa's tobacco pack house (built circa 1947)

The tobacco sticks would be saved from year to year, and before each barn was filled, we'd go to the pack house and get a load of about three or four hundred sticks. We tied them in bundles of 25 each. (My dad would want to know how many sticks we used when working with the green tobacco). We'd put as much cured tobacco as we could into the burlap bags and still be able to tie the corners into the middle of the pile. The bags usually weighed somewhere close to 200 pounds each.

I remember well, spending the mornings working with the green tobacco from the field, going to the house for dinner (and sometimes a short nap), then heading to the packhouse to start working with the cured tobacco. Sometimes we didn't finish the crop until after school started in September, so we had to go to the packhouse and work in the cured tobacco for a few hours, and still somehow get our homework done. I remember a time when the start of the school year was delayed because farmers needed their children to help finish getting the crop out of the field and into the barn.

Cured tobacco (photo courtesy of Billy Wagner)

After a barnful of cured tobacco was packed in the open burlap bags, we backed the *old yeller* Dodge pickup, or the red GMC, down to the packhouse and us kids would lift the bags of tobacco into the loft opening and let it fall into the back of the truck. It was then taken to the tobacco market, a giant warehouse close to town, where buyers came from the tobacco companies, and walked up and down the aisles of *bright leaf* tobacco –– bright, because the highest quality cured tobacco was a golden color and sold for more money.

Buyers would *chant* an auction price and the highest bidder got the tobacco. We'd get to the warehouse very early in the morning, sometimes before 6:00 a.m. and get our vehicle in line behind other people waiting to get into the warehouse and unload. There were times when we arrived even earlier, depending on what else we had to do that day. I remember sleeping in the truck sometimes, and it was not comfortable.

Finally, after an arduously long wait, it was our turn. We'd unload our prize tobacco onto the scales and it was carted away to the warehouse floor by local seasonal workers. After the auction, we headed to the ticket office where the number of pounds and price per pound was calculated and the checks were issued. It was a long process!

When we were finally paid, Mom took charge of the money and deposited it into hers and Dad's joint checking account, and she began to pay bills. There was the fertilizer bill, insecticide and sucker control bills, bills for chemicals to prevent blue mold, and gas for curing, maintenance bills for the tractors, and labor costs. Sometimes we had to borrow from a local bank at the beginning of the tobacco season, and repay the bank when we sold our tobacco.

I remember Mom one time exclaiming, "Bills, bills, bills, that's about all we've got here!"

Mom just headed off to the bank to pay the loans and other bills. Most of the people we owed operated local businesses, so we just started at one end of town and made our way to the other end, writing checks as we went! Sometimes there was a fair amount of money left over, sometimes not. That's why we all had summer jobs, and also why Dad worked in the local textile mill.

In the old days, when I was about ten or eleven years old, farmers had to *grade* the tobacco leaves. The old pack house where we graded our tobacco is still standing now, but just barely. It is gradually being swallowed up by the earth beneath it. The second floor is almost at ground level. All of the water from almost eighty years of rain and melted snow has run straight down the yard and soaked into the ground around the building. In hindsight, there should have been some sort of diversion for the runoff, and the building could have stood another fifty years.

Since there was no electricity in the pack house, we ran a *drop cord* suspended on poles along the way from the house to have a light in the building. In earlier times, people used kerosene lamps. We sometimes worked there until 10:00 or 11:00 p.m.

In the earlier days of tobacco farming, and when I was about six or seven years old, I watched Mom and Grandma grade tobacco. Us kids would help pull the cured leaves off the tobacco stick and Mom and Grandma would make different grades of the leaves depending on the depth of color. One pile had the brightest leaves, another had the next darkest color, and so on. When it was all graded, they would take a handful of leaves and find the very brightest leaf and wrap it around the top of the bundle and tuck the stem end of the leaf through the middle of the bundle. The process was repeated and the bundles were stacked on a tobacco basket, furnished by the warehouse. I remember being so sleepy some nights that I just crawled onto a stack of tobacco and went to sleep.

In the late 1960s, the method of processing cured tobacco changed. A round cardboard hoop was used to place over a burlap bag, and cured tobacco was placed with the stems facing outward until the hoop was filled. We usually tried to get about 200 pounds per bag and then tied the bags corner to corner. We had a set of scales in the packhouse to ensure we had the correct weight.

It was a long, arduous process that was repeated over and over until the last leaves were pulled off the stalks, and they lay bare in the frosty days of October. We then drove the tractor into the field and tilled the empty stalks under the soil. The stalks provided extra nitrogen for the soil and helped get the following year's crop established. It was quite a sight to see acres of bare green sticks where leaves once were, leaves so thick that you couldn't see a person standing in the field if they were very far from you.

Tobacco usually yielded several hundred dollars per acre when we were growing up. After the bank loans were repaid, we usually had enough money to pay off the charge account at the local country store, pay for staples we needed during the growing season, buy a few clothes for the next school year, and catch up on other bills. I don't ever remember getting more than a hundred dollars for the full summer's work on other people's farms in late 60s and early 70s. Of course we didn't get paid for working on my parents' farm. We earned our keep though!

In my sophomore year in high school, I took a class in Agriculture and became a member of Future Farmers of America. I had an official jacket with FFA emblazoned on the back, and my name on the front. It was quite a big deal to have your own jacket and be a member of the club! However, I had no intention of ever becoming a future farmer!

As an FAA member, I had the choice of growing a crop or raising livestock, and since I was already familiar with tobacco production, I chose that as my project. I really had no interest in either one! For my project I kept track of the costs of labor, fertilizer and other chemicals used to grow one acre of tobacco. I had to determine whether I had made a profit or loss after the crop was sold in the fall. I met with the agriculture teacher, Mr. Crews, three times during the summer to review my progress. A written summary of the project was required, as well as accounting ledgers. As I recall, I did make a small profit on my venture. Mr. Crews was pleased, and I received a good grade! As I think back to this time in my life, I'm sure this endeavor provided the discipline I needed to complete projects in college or at work.

By the end of a long, hot, miserable working summer, I would have accumulated about a hundred dollars (when I was about 10-12 years old). Part of that income was attributed to doing other jobs for neighbors. The last years I worked in tobacco, when I was in my late teen's, I would earn as much as three or four hundred dollars each season. I would spend some of that money to buy school clothes, usually checkered shirts and denim pants. I'd also spend some money on film for my camera, but I made sure to save a good portion of my earnings. I had my own bank account, and it was a matter of greatest pride for me to buy as many of my clothes as possible. I was contributing to the family, learning the value of a hard work ethic, and helping to take care of those I loved the most by reducing the financial burden on them any way I could.

Most of the old ways of tobacco farming have been replaced as of this writing. Tobacco plants are now grown in greenhouses instead of in a bed on a piece of farm land. The old log barns are not used anymore for curing, except maybe for farm demonstrations at county fairs, or homestead reenactments for historical purposes. There is an old farm close to my hometown called Duke Homestead in Durham, North Carolina which has yearly reenactments of tobacco production.

Log barns have been replaced by *bulk barns*. These are metal buildings with racks inside to hold the green tobacco. After curing, the tobacco is baled, sort of like baling hay, and then sent directly to the contracted tobacco buyer. Most tobacco production has been highly commercialized nowadays. Countless log barns are sitting abandoned all over the tobacco states, also known as the tobacco belt. Fortunately, in Halifax County there was a state historical grant in recent years that provided funding for the basic restoration of a limited number of these barns. Most of the restored barns are close enough to country roads where they are visible to passersby and tourists. It's a shame that they all couldn't be restored for historical purposes.

All my life, working in tobacco fields and in textile mills has been the standard against which I measured myself. Once I left the farm and started working for companies in California, no matter how bad my job got, how miserable I might feel, how mean my supervisor might be, or the one instance where I was fired from a job that I disliked anyway, I've always reminded myself that what I was doing was better than working in a hot, dirty, tobacco field, pack house or barn. Even digging ditches, cutting wood or shoveling snow was better! At least I would have been in the open, fresh air and not exposed to chemicals. I say this from a historical perspective; tobacco was a big part of our lives and contributed greatly to our livelihood. It was also a simpler time — a time when families worked together, and a time to build our work ethic, so this is what I'd like to remember about my time working in tobacco and textiles.

My parents always told us that they wanted us to get a good education, but it was tobacco that made their words real. Tobacco, and textiles to a lesser degree, and my parents, are what convinced me that I wanted to go to college, to have a career, which eventually involved social work and an office job. No way did I want tobacco (or textiles) to be my only future option. However, I am truly grateful for the lessons that growing tobacco taught me. I wish children of today had the opportunity to get such valuable experience. And I never want to see another tobacco field again!

Early Schooling

School was always important to me. Mom told me that I started first grade at Cluster Springs Elementary School, the very same school that she attended from 1935 through 1942. One building housed first through eighth grade, and another section housed ninth through twelfth grade.

Cluster Springs Elementary (circa early 1940s). Mom's school and where I attended first grade

Mom attended school through grade seven. As I have related earlier, some of the more well-off classmates taunted her because she didn't have nice clothes or makeup. Because of the bullying, she begged my grandparents to let her stay home, and they did. After all, there was plenty of work to do on the farm. Nice clothes and makeup were not important to Mom; getting an education was what mattered. Mom was a very intelligent person. If she'd had half a chance, I'm sure she would have graduated.

After I finished first grade in 1961, the elementary students moved to a new building a few miles down the road. I don't actually remember attending the old wood-framed school. My first recollection of elementary school is 3rd or 4th grade. The original school building still stands today. It has been remodeled, and is located next to, and is used by, the volunteer fire department.

My dad attended Maple Grove School, a one-room elementary school located two miles south of where our home was. He related to me that he only finished the sixth grade. The school building is still standing, surrounded by a grove of trees, and completely wrapped in vines. It looks like something out of a science fiction movie. The ravages of time are evident on the parts that are still visible. It's a historic building that, like a lot of old buildings, most likely will never see restoration. The individual who owns the property adjacent to the school also owns the school property.

While attending elementary school, one emotional event stands out in my mind — the assassination of President John F. Kennedy in November of 1963. I was nine years old and in the fourth grade. It was recess and all the kids were on the playground. I remember the teachers coming out to get us and trying to explain that President Kennedy had been shot. It was tragic and hard for a nine-year-old to make sense of. I remember feeling very sad, and not able to understand how something like this could happen in our country. Although I was physically far removed from the event, it had a profound effect on me at the time. Years later, after moving to California, I had the chance to travel to

Texas and visit the Texas School Book Depository and Dealey Plaza where the assassination occurred. In my mind, I was transported back to my fourth-grade playground and re-hearing the news. It is something that I'll never forget.

My brothers and I attended Cluster Springs until I was to start the sixth grade. At that time, we were attending the Seventh-Day Adventist Church in South Boston. Mom thought it best at the time to send us to a private Christian school that was operated by our church. The school was located in Danville, Virgina, 40 miles west of where we lived. So, for the next two and a half years, a member of the church drove my three brothers and myself, along with three members of another family, back and forth from South Boston to Danville. We would have to be ready to go each morning by 7:30 a.m. and usually got home around 4:30 p.m.

One day while playing softball at recess, a schoolmate hit a ball directly into my face and broke my nose. I had to spend two days in the local hospital. My nose had to be pushed back into place. Nowadays a person would get taped up and sent home the same day!

When I went home from the hospital, my friends wanted to go to the local country store for a soda. When the store owner's three-year-old son saw me, he ran behind the counter yelling, "Mama, mama, Batman's gonna get me!" The doctor at the hospital had put tape across my nose in an *X* shape and I guess I looked like Batman. It was hard enough for me to go out in public with tape all over my face, let alone deal with a poor kid scared out of his wits! We hurriedly made our purchase and left.

After recovering, I returned to school and my classmates gave me a money tree as a welcome back gift, and the principal made a speech about how lucky I was that the injury wasn't more serious. The incident had a lasting effect on me though. I played softball some after this, but from that time forward I was always afraid to be the pitcher in a game. I guess I should have learned to put the glove in front of my face!

I also remember performing in school plays. The one play that stands out had to do with students dressing up as vegetables. Because I was so tall, I was elected to be a stalk of celery. I remember being so embarrassed in front of the crowd who came to see us perform. I think it was more to teach about eating habits than performing in a real play.

After two and a half years, it became too expensive for us to attend the Christian school, so we were re-enrolled in public schools. By then I was almost thirteen years old. At that time, grades eight through twelve were all in one school, Halifax County High School. I remember not fitting in very well after being in a smaller, more sheltered environment. I quickly became the brunt of harassment. It was common for kids who were introverted to get ridiculed. Nothing was ever done about it because things would only get worse, so I kept focused on my studies. I took all the basic subjects until my junior year. At that point I realized that if I wanted to go to college, I'd need to take some more advanced subjects. I enrolled in first year French, Geometry, Chemistry, English and Government. I remember going home and locking myself in my room with my books. It was the only way I could have enough quiet time in order to do my homework. I never neglected my studies, no matter what else I had to do. They came first. I knew that if I ever wanted to pursue something different from farm life I'd have to push myself.

I remember going to the local library to get books for English book reports. In 1971 the local library consisted of several small crowded rooms in a converted Craftsman home. However, I could usually find whatever I needed there. A new library was built in 1979 which was considerably larger, and contained a greater collection of books. I'd read parts of books for my English reports, but never really completed an entire book. I had a problem concentrating on my reading. It wasn't that I couldn't read well, it was that my attention span was short. I remember having to read and re-read material throughout high school, and later on in college. When a paper was due, I'd go to a local shop that rented typewriters and other business machines. I thought maybe if I typed my reports, I'd get a better grade, but more credit was given to how one wrote, rather than if it was handwritten or typed. One report I remember writing was the account of the Apollo moon landing in 1969. I went out and bought a newspaper, read the story, cut out the pictures and wrote a report in my own words. Of course, I watched the landing on our old RCA black and white TV, the one with the rabbit ears and tin foil!

I also recall how strange it was taking a French class. I remember how an opportunity to travel to Paris came about in 1972, my senior year of high school, but I could not afford the trip. In hindsight, I might have been able to raise the money. I had the idea of putting a sad picture of me on a jar and placing it in the country store, detailing my desire to travel, and asking for donations. I probably would have received only a few pennies! I don't think my parents would have allowed me to get on an airplane and fly thousands of miles away anyway. It was the chance of a lifetime that I missed. Here I was, never having been exposed to much of any kind of culture, learning to speak another language. It was one of many things that I wanted to do in order to learn how other people lived.

It took me a long time to discover that there were cultural events going on in the world around me, but I was so constrained by the life that had been built for me, and around me, that it was hard to step out of that confinement. In that area of the country, there were certain things that were expected of us. We would work on the farm and get a basic education, usually meaning high school. After high school, we were expected to find a full-time job, get married, buy a house and raise a family. Those are things that the average person aspires to do, and there's nothing wrong with that. However, most people I knew growing up stayed in the *bubble* and never ventured very far away or experienced the cultural aspects of life. For the most part, they also followed the political leanings of their parents. It was a generational thing. I think there was, to some extent, the fear of the unknown, and at the same time, the desire to be complacent, or fit into the proper *mold*. It would have been very easy just to do the basics and compromise to what life was like there. However, if your family was well-known, influential or wealthy, then your children had a better opportunity of improving their status. In my family, however, we were somewhat constrained by expectations and financial ability.

At that time, I had never been exposed to classical music or art, and had finished high school without ever having seen a museum. To most of my family and acquaintances, there wasn't much need for cultural things, and even today, the same concept mostly holds true, even though the area now has a historical museum and a performing arts center. That is great progress!

One thing I did as soon as I reached voting age was to participate in the political process. It became one of the most important aspects of my idea of freedom and change, and remains so today. South-Central, rural Virginia is very conservative, and has been as long as I can remember. If your parents voted one way, everyone else in the family voted the same way. Except for me! In 1972, when I was eighteen, I cast my first vote for the Democratic party. I never told anyone until many years later, because I knew I'd get stares and disapprovals. My family was no exception; they voted for conservatives, and they went to church (but on Saturday instead of Sunday).

In my hometown in the early 1980s, there were so-called *Blue Laws*, where you couldn't buy or sell any merchandise on Sunday until after 12:00 noon, and the purchase of alcohol on Sunday was strictly prohibited. I remember one particular issue, liquor by the drink, being placed on the ballot for a vote. Religious organizations came out in full force, protesting with signs in our little downtown. Needless to say, it did not pass. Some years later, in the late 1980s, it did eventually pass.

There are more liberals living in South Boston now, and a more diverse population, but still not enough to turn the tide, and the mindset for my age group (Baby Boomers) remains pretty much the same now as when we were children. Liberal ideas don't get much traction. Hopefully one day this will eventually even out. In the meantime, I'd like to point out that I prefer to debate the issues instead of putting politics over family and friends. By understanding and considering others' opinions, we can help foster relationships, build trust, and strengthen connections with friends, family and colleagues.

When I graduated from high school, I was the first member of my family to do so. My parents never finished elementary school. Two of my brothers never finished high school. My youngest brother (Carl) and I are the only family members to do so, myself in 1972, and Carl in 1976. On the night of my graduation, I borrowed my oldest brother's car and Mom and I attended the ceremony. I had strict instructions from my brother to return his car promptly after graduation, so I was not able to attend any graduation celebrations. No one in my family ever went to college; I was the first one to attend.

Race Relations and Desegregation

In 1954 the Supreme Court ruled in *Brown v. Board of Education* that "schools segregated by race did not provide an equal education." Due to many years of anti-desegregation court cases, the schools in Halifax County were not desegregated until 1970. I was in my sophomore year in high school, and remember how students in both the white and Black high schools were given two weeks off, sometime in March of that year. This was to allow for records and people to be transferred. When we returned to classes, the makeup of each high school was mostly 50/50 Black and white. My youngest brother was four years younger than myself, so he was assigned to attend the former Black high school, which then housed grades eight and nine after integration.

The integration in Halifax County was largely achieved through busing. Being a rural farming area, there was really no other way to do it. Some kids were fortunate enough to own vehicles, but my brothers and I rode the bus. I remember it being loud and crowded. Sometimes fights broke out, not so much between Black and white, but mostly between white kids. The bus driver would have to pull over and break up the fight and get their names for disciplinary action.

I recently came across an online news item in *neaToday* that discussed Professor Vanessa Siddle Walker's research on school integration. She explains that after integration:

…there was widespread dismissal, demotion, or forced resignation of tens of thousands of experienced, highly credentialed Black teachers and principals who staffed the Black only schools. After schools were integrated, many white superintendents in the southern U.S. who were against integration in the first place were unwilling to put Black educators in positions of authority over white teachers or students (…) "Black educators discovered that they were the victims of an exchange model through which they traded *aspiration* and *advocacy* for access to the resources white schools had." ("A Hidden History of Integration and the Shortage of Teachers of Color," *nea Today*, Long, Cindy, 3/11/20).

As a result, Black history got lost in the shuffle. In the years to follow, some of the advocacy and history was restored through efforts of the Civil Rights movement. Today we see those efforts being slowly eroded away by state legislatures all over the country. Some state governments are trying to stifle diversity, equity and inclusion. In fact, the federal government has now begun to remove references to *DEI* from the policies of its agencies. A different version of Black history is being taught. I am fortunate that during my educational process, I have heard the *correct* version of that history.

The integration of both Black and white students in my hometown went very smoothly. I can't recall any violent episodes occurring. Actually, I had more Black friends in high school than white friends. In fact, on the farm, we worked side by side with both Black and white neighbors. There was one family in particular I remember very well — the Hall family. They were hard workers and we could always depend on them. The mother's name was *Mamie*. She greeted everyone with a broad smile; her kind eyes pierced through you and warmed your soul! We were always respectful of each other. No racial remarks were allowed in their presence, and my family was respectful when not in their presence. However, I do remember when our Black friends were not around, some white people would make disparaging remarks, to which I always took offense and stood up for them!

Many of my Black high school friends went on to obtain Master's and Doctorates because they knew that education was the key to pulling themselves out of poverty. It's a shame though that they couldn't have had the same resources in the all-Black schools as were in the all-white schools, prior to integration.

Early College Days

When I finished high school in 1972, I immediately enrolled at Danville Community College, which was forty miles west of where I lived. It was quite a drive back and forth, four days a week, eighty miles round trip. I used money I had saved to purchase gas and meals, as long as it lasted, and then my parents chipped in. For one year my cousin and I did ride-share. She would drive one week and I the next.

I did not want to burden my parents with the costs of college, so I applied for a few local scholarships. I was selected by a local bank which was the administrator for a fund that was earmarked for low-income college students. The scholarship paid for two years of tuition and books at the school I selected.

In the beginning, I chose Data Processing as my major. I remember having to learn COBOL and FORTRAN programming, which was very difficult for me. Back in the *ancient days*, all the data we used, including the computer language, had to be handwritten on a data input sheet, and subsequently keyed onto punch cards using a key-punch machine. If any of the computer language was incorrect, the program (job) would not run correctly. At that point, I would have to go through stacks of punch cards and find the language mistake, re-key the card with the mistake, and then resend all the cards through a card reader machine. The data was then transmitted to a mainframe at a nearby university in Richmond, Virginia. If the data was correct, it was retransmitted to my school and printed on the old green and white striped paper. My final project for the first year was to compute the wages earned and all the payroll deductions for a company of fifty employees. After a few attempts, the project was successful. Nowadays, we take for granted that the language that drives a computer program is running in the background on all our modern-day devices. We get instantaneous information on our desktops, laptops and in the palms of our hands.

In my second year at Danville Community College, I decided to change my major to Business Management; I'd had such a tough time with Data Processing. This new program was more of a bookkeeping role and was a bit less stressful than the earlier program. I remember using adding machines in class that were as big as a small microwave! So much progress has been made in the computer and business field since my first attempt at college in 1972. Driving eighty miles a day and taking a full course load was not an easy task.

After starting two different programs, I would have had to attend another year in Business Management in order to graduate. Hence, I did not graduate from Community College at that time (1974). I felt pressure to find a job after two years in two different programs. I still wasn't sure which way I wanted to go career-wise, so I stopped attending school and started looking for a job. I realize now that this was a big mistake. I should have continued school at that point and obtained a bachelor's degree. As a result, I spent many years working jobs that I wasn't happy with. (As a footnote, one of my first professors in the Data Processing program has kept in touch with me over the years).

Early Employment

My first public job was at a furniture plant called Daystrom Furniture. It was a job that required the worker to punch a time card when they started work, again at lunch, and finally at the end of the shift. I was hired for a second-shift job, working from 3:00 p.m. to 11:00 p.m., sanding the edges of newly-constructed kitchen chair bottoms as they came off a conveyor belt. On my second night of work, the supervisor asked the machine operator how I was doing on the job. My co-worker said that I was doing great. The supervisor replied, "Speed it up Charlie!" Looking back, this reminds me of the *I Love Lucy* episode where Lucy and Ethel are working in the candy factory, and their supervisor speeded up the conveyor belt. Needless to say, they could not keep up. And neither could I! Their candy was not getting processed just as the chair bottoms were not getting sanded. In my case the chair bottoms piled up on the floor!

The supervisor's office was located up near the ceiling so they had a 360-degree view of the entire plant floor and everyone in it. We were watched every minute of our shift. I wore out a pair of gloves every night and went home with blisters on my hands. I had to practically beg for a new pair of gloves each night. Misery was my only companion on that job! I worked only three nights and quit! It was a non-union job, as most jobs were in the 1970s. My co-worker was shocked when I told him that I thought I could do better than working at a furniture plant. Not that I thought I deserved better, but that I thought I was intelligent enough to do better. The plant eventually closed about the time that other manufacturing companies in the area closed, in the late 1990s and early 2000s.

J. P. Stevens Textile Mill

After being traumatized at the furniture plant job, I found a job at the same textile mill that my dad and most of his family worked for. My dad had *strongly encouraged* me to apply. It was called J. P. Stevens. This textile mill was built in my hometown sometime around 1940. Just about every family I knew worked there. Halifax County was home to a cotton mill, a synthetics mill (where I worked), and a *worsted* plant where wool products were produced.

I started working at Stevens in 1977. This company had been around since the mid-1850s, and started in Landover, Massachusetts before the mills started moving south, where there was an abundance of cheap labor, primarily women and children. Cotton crops were located in the South, so having the mills in proximity to the labor force was advantageous. Gradual improvements in machinery created more efficiency and kept labor costs down. The company used synthetic yarn and processed it into woven fabric. Most of the fabric we produced was for women's apparel. There were some fabrics that were produced for military purposes, but they were discontinued because the women's apparel industry was more profitable.

My hours were from 12:00 midnight to 8:00 a.m. It was a hot and sweaty job. There was air conditioning, but it sometimes broke down and we became miserable! With all the yarn whirling around, I'm sure filaments and dust were flying through the air, and we were breathing it in.

There were many different processes that the yarn went through to prepare it for weaving. My job was called *Creeling*. Generally speaking, I set up spools of yarn on frames, and a machine operator ran the yarn through a giant comb and onto a large metal spool, called a *beam*. The machine was called a *warper*. And believe me, sometimes this machine ran at warp speeds, not unlike some of the vehicles in science fiction TV shows! Most of the time I could barely keep enough yarn set up to keep the machine running.

Example of a Draper-type loom used in weaving at JPS (circa early 1980s)

The number of threads corresponded to the requirement of whatever type of fabric was being woven. Several of the large beams were taken to another processing area, run through a starch-like solution, and combined onto one or more beams. Each thread of yarn was then *drawn* through a reed (large comb) and heddles, or looped wires with holes in the end for the warped yarn to travel through, and to be separated. Once this process was completed, the beam was then mounted on a loom to begin the weaving process. There were large rooms full of looms. When they were all operating and weaving, the noise was deafening!

This was a very challenging time in my life. Looking back, I appreciate the fact that I had a job, and I appreciate that this company provided a livelihood for so many people for over a half century. However, I felt like this job, like working in tobacco, was a complete dead end for me. There was no opportunity to advance because people who landed better jobs stayed on those jobs until retirement. I felt as though I was quite capable of doing most any job in the factory. I wanted to do something different with my life, and I realized at the time that I'd need to get a better education if I was ever going to find what I wanted to do.

There was a manager whom I got to know very well, and he let me fill in for several weeks in the office on two different occasions (over the thirteen years that I worked there). He saw potential in me based on my work ethic; for that I am grateful. Over the years since the mill closed, we have kept in touch. The duties were mostly clerical, but it beat laboring and sweating out on the factory floor. Being completely honest, I never tried to *buddy* with supervisors or other workers in order to get easier work assignments, although I was accused of it by some co-workers. I gave an honest day's work, just like I had been taught to do by my parents.

Except for the few months of working in the office, I was pushed to the limit on every shift! I had some good co-workers, and some who didn't take their job seriously. If my job did happen to get caught up, I would be assigned to work my job as well as help co-workers who were behind on their jobs. Consequently, my job would then get behind. It was a tough time in my life. I suspect that some workers had easier jobs than others because they knew someone important in management.

I recall a coworker who had an easier job than myself, and she would disappear for long periods of time. One night my supervisor asked if I had seen her, and I simply pointed to a large, four-foot box sitting in the corner. He looked in the box and there she was, reading a book. They both had a good laugh as I kept toiling away. There were no consequences. There were others that sometimes came to work intoxicated, but it was overlooked. Some of these workers were operating machinery! Unions were practically unheard of, and I remember indirectly being discouraged from joining one.

In the 1970s and 1980s smoking was allowed on the job. When I look back at this period in my life, things sure have changed. Nowadays smoking isn't allowed in work areas or near buildings. Our breaks were twenty minutes for lunch or dinner, and two ten-minute breaks in between. I pretty much stayed to myself during work and during breaks. There really wasn't time for talking. I remember going home at 8:00 a.m. and not being able to sleep, wondering what the next night would be like. I could hear the clatter, clatter and the whirling of the machines in my mind, even after being awake for sixteen hours.

A few years before I left the textile mill, the work shift changed from eight hours to twelve hours, and the mill was open twenty-four hours a day, seven days a week. This was a way to cut down on overtime pay. Looking back, it may have been a way to keep the operation running for a few extra years, but in the end, it would not prove to be enough to withstand foreign competition.

There were some good times, and some not so good, but it was an experience I will never forget. I look at it now as an experience that helped shape me into becoming the person I am today.

Christmastime was always a nice time at the plant. When we were kids, I remember the company bringing truckloads of packaged toys and fruit to the plant. Most of the time, the toys we received at the textile mill were the only toys we received for Christmas. Of course, our parents gave us clothes, shoes and other necessities. There would also be a nice meal for everyone. There was a sense of community and belonging among the employees, and a sense of pride in the work we had accomplished during the year. I too shared in that camaraderie, even though it wasn't the job I had envisioned for my future.

There were also gifts given to employees for maintaining per-fect attendance, and also service awards. During my thirteen years of employment with the mill, I was able to maintain perfect attendance for five consecutive years. I still have an *exquisite* faux-wood mantle clock and a couple of throw rugs as a reminder of my employment there! Looking back, I think I should have taken more days off, maybe I would have had a slightly better disposition.

There were some other positive things that the mill was involved in, such as the Red Cross blood drive. Countless employees donated each year. Also, assistance was given to local youth baseball leagues. There was a ball field down the street from the mill where kids played. Some employees also donated time to the Chamber of Commerce and other community support groups. Fundraising for the United Way was always a big commitment for most employees.

Unions were practically unheard of in the South; our plant was no exception. If there had been a union, people would have received higher wages, better working conditions and better healthcare, but all at a greater expense for the company, along with the risk of labor force reductions. I remember leaving work at 8:00 a.m. after a long graveyard shift, and seeing union representatives near the front parking lot. They weren't allowed in the building. They carried signs identifying their union. Most people sped by the representatives and refused to take the literature. Being afraid of potentially losing my job, unfortunately I did the same thing. There have been movies made, such as *Norma Rae,* that depict life in the textile mills, and they are pretty accurate in their descriptions!

J. P. Stevens, South Boston, VA textile plant (circa 1980)

I was constantly looking in the local paper for other jobs the entire time I worked for J.P. Stevens. The issue was that I only had a high school education, and had never completed college. And after working a grueling eight or twelve-hour shift, if I did happen to see a job opening of interest, I felt I didn't have the energy to go on an interview. What usually happened is that individuals who had college degrees got whatever scarce openings that became available. I also tried local government, but I always lacked qualifications, or didn't know my congressional representative or my district board of supervisor's member well enough to get a recommendation. I got locked into my job at J.P. Stevens because I needed to work. Although I had a good work history, a good work ethic and excellent references, I always lacked the specific qualifications for a better job. I received responses from prospective employers, but they were always the turn-down type of response. Hmm, education must have been the key!

Over the years I was occasionally laid off a week at a time and received unemployment. The company called it *rotating out*. Incidentally, unemployment was about as much as I made working. I remember starting out in 1977 at about $1.50 per hour, and when I finally left the textile mill thirteen years later, in 1990, I was making less than $5.00 per hour! Although I was not happy with my job, the positive thing that I took away from my time at a textile mill is that I was able to further establish my work ethic, which served as a huge reinforcement for me in subsequent jobs.

I visited the Boott Cotton Mills Museum, Lowell, Massachusetts in 2011 (weaving demonstration)

J.P. Stevens went out of business in 2001 primarily due to foreign competition. Many people staked their livelihoods in this company, so when it ceased to exist, people had few opportunities, other than working in fast-food, or retail stores like Walmart. Over the years the company provided employment for a lot of people, including myself. I made enough money to make payments on my first home I bought in 1986. I remember J.P. Stevens now in a nostalgic and historical context. It's an important part of my history, and the history of our community at large for which it served, and it deserves recognition. It was once a stalwart in the county. However, it is ironic, and sad to say the least, that the building where so many people made an honest living has been torn down, and is now reduced to nothing more than a pile of rubble in an overgrown thicket!

The Dump and the Junk Man

My grandpa in his infinite wisdom decided to sell eight to ten acres of their farm on which we lived to the county. This was in the 1960s. The county needed property on which to construct a landfill. Workers pushed down trees and built a dirt road from the main two-lane highway on which we lived. This road passed within a few hundred yards of our house. The landfill was approximately a quarter of a mile into my grandparent's property. At the end of the dirt road, they dug huge ditches across the property, and put gravel down on the road and in front of the ditches, so vehicles wouldn't get stuck when it rained. They placed huge poles, like telephone poles, in front of the ditches to prevent people from backing their vehicles into this giant precipice.

People would drive to the dump and discard their own garbage because there was no county trash pick-up. Traffic was miserable! On hot summer days, dust clouds from the vehicles traveling to and from the dump would swirl all around us and obscure our view. It would choke off your breath if you were sitting on the back porch of our house. During the hot summer months, the county would dispatch a tanker truck full of water and spray the road to contain the dust. That didn't last but a day or two. So, what happened? When it rained, people were afraid to go all the way to the ditches to discard their trash, because sometimes, even with gravel on the road, they would get stuck in the mud! People began dumping their refuse in the middle of the road. Sometimes we could even see the ever-encroaching pile of trash from our back door! Eventually, after much complaining, and a period of relatively dry weather, the county pushed the trash back to where it was supposed to be. The same scenario repeated itself many times over the five years that the dump was there.

Believe it or not, the dump was not all bad. There was poor-folk trash and rich-folk trash. The rich folks would throw away things that we never imagined we could have for free! So, what did we do? Remember, we were poor kids in the 1960s, so this was exciting stuff! My brothers and myself, along with childhood friends, went treasure hunting!

We spent untold hours searching through the rubble of other people's lives. We found coins, sometimes bags full of pennies, and even collectible items such as glassware, silverware, even dolls! We found clothes that looked like they'd hardly been worn, and items of furniture that, when cleaned up, looked as good as new! I remember finding an antique trunk and a mantle clock that still worked.

At the time, in order to supplement their income, Mom, Grandma and one of Mom's sisters, were collecting aluminum cans, copper wire and other metal that could be sold to the *junk man*. This was a guy who was in business to buy these items for a small amount. He would then resell them to a recycler for a profit. Sometimes the junk man would drive his big truck down the road where we lived. If we saw him, we would get him to stop at our house and pick up the junk we'd found. Otherwise, we'd have to transport it to his business location. We didn't care. It was free money! Every time our childhood friends came for a visit, we'd ride our bikes to the dump and go searching for treasure!

Five years after opening, the dump became full and a new location had to be found. Everyone who lived in the area was relieved! Us kids were kind of sad that our fun had been taken away, not to mention the extra money we were making. However, we still could ride our bikes up and down the dirt road. Many years later, the land along the *dump* road was sold, and there are currently four families living there, including one of my brothers. When we talk, we still refer to the road as the *dump road*.

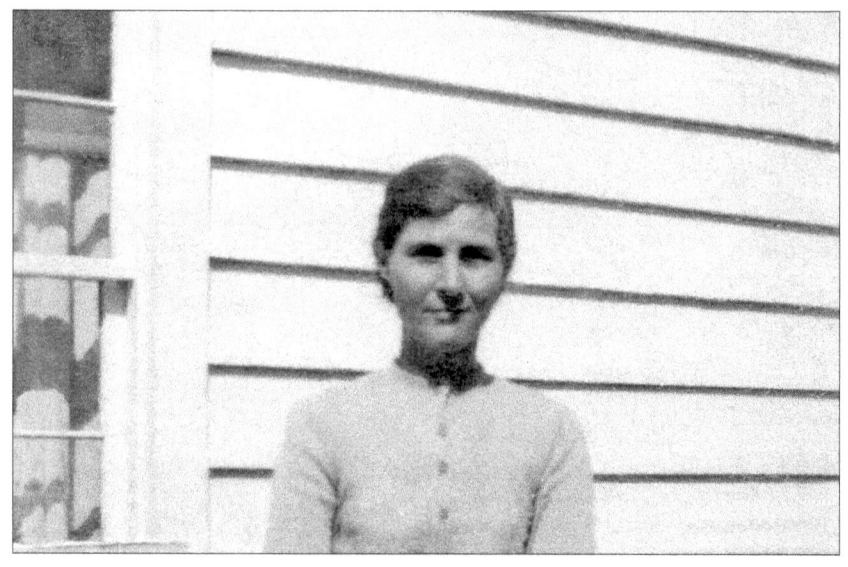

My grandma (circa 1947)

Grandma

My maternal grandmother Maryland Keaton Newton was a very kind, soft-spoken lady who had a very hard upbringing. She was born in 1905 in the poor rural community of Mecklenburg, Virginia. Her mother passed away when she was only five years old. Her dad re-married and soon she had five brothers and a sister. Grandma related to me how she was required to do a lot of the housework. At five years old, her step-mom would put a bench for her to stand on at the kitchen sink because she was not tall enough to wash the dishes. Grandma was like Cinderella without the glass slippers.

Grandma Newton never had any formal education. She often related to me that this was very common amongst most poor farm families of her generation. She basically taught herself to read and write by asking a lot of questions of other family members, and friends who were literate. She was expected to stay home and help with cleaning, washing clothes and preparing meals. She was married when she was twenty-one, although some girls got married at age fifteen or sixteen, and already bore children by the time they were eighteen. Grandma was good at finances too. She managed to save money, even though times were hard. I am certain that she denied herself a lot of the things that we all take for granted.

From the time I was a little kid, I remember Grandma being thrifty with her money. She received Social Security, but prior to that she worked as a Nurse's Aide. She had a secret hiding place where she stashed her savings. I don't think she fully trusted the banks. The hiding place was in the kitchen pantry. There was a cutout in the wall at the ceiling, and she had a box of some sort, maybe a cigar box, where she kept her cash money. I never tried to find the hiding place, but I remember her going in the pantry and coming out with a few dollars in her hand. She tried to give me money when I'd drive her and Grandpa places, but I always refused. She would just drop it in the car seat when she got out.

When Grandma passed away in 1997, I remember relatives talking about the money that she saved had gone missing, and that they thought she had buried it somewhere in the backyard. I mentioned that she had the secret hiding place in the pantry, and a less than scrupulous family member tore a small portion of the drywall out of the pantry looking for the money. One relative went so far as to take a shovel and dig around Grandma's favorite tree. Relatives also looked under the house and inside the old well. The well was one that had been dug by hand, and had buckets connected to a chain and a pulley. To my knowledge the money was never found. Maybe the money was put in the well bucket and let down into the water. Or more likely, the money was spent or just didn't exist.

Grandma also had several pieces of antique furniture, and an oval-framed picture of my great uncle Fitzhugh who served in WW I. Most of those pieces of furniture went to relatives, but an oak dresser that was over a hundred years old and the oval-framed picture went missing. To this day I regret not asking for that picture, and I regret not sitting with Grandma to get every detail of her upbringing and her marriage. A lot of family history is lost because we don't think it's important when we're young. But when we're older it becomes more and more significant. It also becomes harder and harder to piece together, because younger family members don't remember things or simply didn't ask. Nowadays, people just don't seem as concerned about preserving family history as they once were.

I have a lot of fond memories of my grandma Newton. She was always making quilts. Grandma and Mom would recycle used clothing and worn-out bed sheets to make the quilts. They'd cut up pieces of fabric according to the different designs they wanted to create, and then sew them together on an old Singer foot-pedal sewing machine. Once the pieces were sewn together, Grandma and Mom would set up quilting frames in Grandma's living room and stitch around each square of fabric by hand. They made some of the most beautiful quilts I've ever seen. They had a talent, a gift that no doubt was passed down from generation to generation. There were designs called Dutch Girl and Dutch Boy, Log Cabin, Doves, Double Wedding Ring, and of course the Crazy Quilt. I am fortunate to have two of the quilts that Mom made. They are family heirlooms, and priceless to me.

At one time, Mom and Grandma were making quilts for a lady who had a retail shop in another county. They were selling the quilts they made for her at a ridiculously low price, and found out later that the shop lady was making a huge profit re-selling the quilts in her store. Needless to say, Mom and Grandma stopped making quilts for this person.

I also remember Grandma's fondness of reading. As I mentioned earlier, Grandma self-taught herself to read and write. She read the local newspaper, flyers that her church produced, and letters from relatives. Most of all I remember her reading her Bible. She was very devoted to her faith and to her church.

Mom quilting in the 1970s

My grandma Newton quilting in the 1970s

Grandma also taught herself to crochet. I never asked her when she started, but I figure she must have been doing this for most of her adult life. When we tied green tobacco to be hung in the barn for curing, we used white tobacco twine. Once the tobacco was cured and taken off the tobacco stick, I remember Grandma picking up the scrap pieces of twine. She would bleach, unravel and then wind the twine into a ball. When she had a good supply of recycled twine, she would start crocheting. I don't remember how long it took, but she eventually made a bedspread that I have as a remembrance of her. It is actually so heavy that you can't turn over in bed if it's on top of you! It is beautiful, and it reminds me of the old saying, *waste not, want not*.

Grandma was also good at gardening. She could grow pretty much anything. I remember seeing her break off parts of flowering plants and propagating them. She'd take a piece of a plant and put it in the soil in a sunny location, and place a quart glass jar over it. Before long, the cutting had roots and she transferred the new plant to a pot, or another location in the yard. I recently tried this myself, and successfully propagated two rose bushes!

She grew several different kinds of fruit in her small orchard including apples. When the apples became ripe and were picked, Grandma would slice them, place them on a cheesecloth, and dry them in the sun. She then stored the dried fruit in large glass jars. Sometime later the dried apples were reconstituted in water and used to make fried apple pies, or half-moon pies as some people call them. Those pies had the best flavor! The ones my grandma made were the best!

Grandma also grew all sorts of vegetables behind the old smokehouse in her back yard. The smokehouse was where they hung meat (usually hogs that had been slaughtered) to be smoked with burning hickory wood. She also had a pantry devoted exclusively to storing her canned goods. In the winter, when we were unable to grow food, those jars of vegetables meant that her family would have good meals.

My grandma Newton's tobacco field behind the smokehouse (early 1960s)

I have a photo of Grandma standing in the garden spot where tobacco was planted. She would put newspapers around the plants and in the middle of the rows to control weeds. She tilled every inch of her garden by hand, up until she was well into her 70s. For watering in dry spells, she had a large metal barrel that sat under the roof drip of the old smokehouse. When it rained, the barrel would usually fill up. She'd then carry buckets of water to use in the garden. She also used the same water to wash her hair. She said that rain water made your hair softer. She was from a generation that didn't waste anything.

Another good memory I have is from Christmastime. We always spent this time of year at Grandma's house. We didn't have tree farms and the stores didn't carry live trees back then, so my brothers (Carl and David) and I scoured the fields on Grandma's property for a tree. We usually chose a cedar tree. We'd cut the tree, then nail a wooden crosspiece to the end so it would stand upright. We had one string of electric lights, some tinsel, and a few old ornaments that we reused year after year. We'd take the Christmas cards that my grandparents had received and tape them around the door in the living room.

Us kids spent more time visiting with Mom's relatives. I only remember Dad taking us to visit my paternal grandmother a few times during my childhood, but occasionally Dad's brothers and sisters would come to our house for short visits. We always enjoyed talking to Dad's brother Owen.

Mom's brother Crawley and his family from North Carolina, Mom's sister Thelma from Richmond, and Mom's sister Laura who lived locally, would all come over for the holidays. And of course, my brothers and I would be there. Dad didn't like large crowds, so he stayed home for most of the holiday gatherings. We would always bring food home to him.

Uncle Crawley was a smart businessman, although he, like his siblings, never completed his basic education. When his three children were young, he operated several automobile service stations in Durham, NC. I admired him for taking such great care of his family, and my grandparents. Uncle Crawley would always make himself available when his help was needed. Before passing in 1993, he owned his own convenience store near his home. One of my fondest memories of him was when he took my brothers and myself for a ride in his red convertible in the mid-1960s. We were going over 100 miles per hour down our country road with the convertible top down. What a thrill that was! He is greatly missed.

Uncle Crawley Christmas 1992

Grandma would fix a big meal, which usually consisted of several vegetables, sometimes chicken or turkey, homemade biscuits and her famous fried apple pies. Grandma's house was full of love and laughter during the holidays. It was a happy time. We didn't have this kind of atmosphere at our house. Unfortunately, a lot of our time at home was spent avoiding our dad. We never knew what his reaction to any given situation would be (more about this later). Of course we had love, but it wasn't expressed as openly as it was at Grandma's house.

Aunt Laura, Aunt Thelma and Mom in Richmond in 2001

In the 1960s and early 1970s, I remember Grandma using a wood-cook stove. Everything cooked on the wood stove seemed to taste so much better. It had a different flavor, richer and more enhanced. Some people say that a bit of smoke from the wood fire finds its way into the food and that changes the taste. When I was six or seven years old, I went to visit Grandma early one morning as she was getting ready to start cooking for the day. I had the idea that I would help her, so I went to the wood pile in the backyard and got some *kindling*. This was wood cut from *knots* in pine trees, and was used as a starter for fires. I came back with the wood, but couldn't seem to get the fire started. Grandma was busy with other chores, so being the bright kid that I was, I spotted a gas can that was used to fill the lawnmower. I poured some in a plastic cup, brought it inside and poured about four ounces over the wood I'd already placed in the stove. I struck a match and whoof! It sounded like an explosion! The fire singed my eyebrows and scared the heck out of me, but otherwise I was okay. Grandma came running and grabbed my arm, jerking me away from the stove. "Don't ever do that again," she said, in a frightened and angry voice. I wouldn't come near her stove after that! I would never be good at camping!

As a kid I recall watching Grandma make homemade lye soap. She used a black, three-legged cast-iron pot, the kind you might see witches in the movies use to brew their concoctions! Grandma built a wood fire in the yard, away from any leaves or dried grass, and had a circle of rocks around the fire area for the pot to sit on so it was elevated above the fire. At the time, people saved grease from cooking meat because it was a key ingredient in soap-making. Grandma heated the grease over the fire for a certain length of time, mixed lye and water into the batch, and then took the pot off the fire to let it cool. When the mixture had cooled, she said that the soap needed to *cure* for a couple of weeks before it would be safe to use. She would then cut the soap into squares, and use it for laundry or washing hands. Lye soap is what I remember using to get the tobacco wax off my hands when we farmed tobacco.

In the mid-1960s, my grandpa Newton had a stroke and was unable to drive or talk coherently. He was around 65 when this happened. I can distinctly recall that his doctor still made house calls at the time.

He was the same doctor that my parents, brothers and I saw when we needed medical attention. Grandpa was eventually able to walk with a walker and get around in the house and outside. I remember Grandma waiting on him faithfully over a period of ten years.

I also helped out when I could. I had bought my first car, a 1962 Chevrolet Impala when I graduated from high school in 1972. From that time on until his passing in 1976, I provided transportation for him and Grandma. My grandma lived another twenty-one years after Grandpa's death. I moved to California in 1990, but would travel back to South Boston quite frequently. Whenever I was back home, I made sure to spend a lot of time with Grandma.

When I'd come home for a visit, Grandma and I would have long conversations while sitting under a big oak tree in her backyard. I treasure those conversations. I have a photograph of her and me under that oak tree. It's funny, I was pretty much the only one who could get her to take a picture at that point in her life.

On one occasion we talked about New Year's traditions in Southern Virginia. For as long as I can remember, we always had a meal of black-eyed peas cooked with ham (or ham hock) and either collard or turnip greens on New Year's Day. Black-eyed peas have been grown in the South for hundreds of years, and are associated with a *mystical* power to bring good luck. Collard and turnip greens are green like money, and supposedly will secure financial success for the year. Throw in some pan-fried cornbread for extra good luck!

Grandma noted that the tradition of eating black-eyed peas dates back to Civil War days. For generations, relatives have passed down this information in her family. It is said that when Northern troops raided farms in the South, black-eyed peas were considered suitable only for animal feed, and were left behind. The poor and enslaved people were grateful to have the peas to eat, and have considered them good luck ever since. The Emancipation Proclamation was ordered by President Lincoln on January 1,1863. From that time forward, people living in the South prepared a meal of black-eyed peas and collards on New Year's Day. I may never have known this information had it not been for my grandma's recollection of family history. Although I no longer live in the South, I continue this tradition.

The last photo taken of Grandma Newton and myself together
(summer of 1996)

Grandma also told me that I should avoid doing laundry or other cleaning on New Year's Day, because doing so would wash away the good luck for the year!

Another thing my grandma spoke about was that her side of the family had Native American blood lines. I have done a little research, but have not been able to verify that. I do regret not sitting down with her and getting more detailed family genealogy. Once the older generation has passed, it is very difficult for younger family members to obtain important family information. One thing I know for sure, she treasured her children and grandchildren, and she was devoted to her family and to her church. She was full of wisdom. I miss her very much.

White Lightning
and *Old Smoky*

My dad, Willie T. Howerton Jr., was born in 1930, right at the beginning of the Depression. He worked for the local Esso gas station in South Boston's Riverdale enclave. Riverdale was, and still is, a crossroads community where two major Virginia highways intersect (one north/south bound, the other east/west). I don't have much information on my dad when he was a child, except for the fact that his dad, my grandpa Willie Howerton Sr., died in a car accident in 1940. He was only forty-one years old, and my dad was 10 when this accident occurred. Dad was the third child of five brothers and three sisters.

My earliest recollection of my dad is from about 1964. That is when he and several of his friends in our community hauled bootleg liquor, *white lightning* if you will, across the North Carolina border into Virginia. This was a felony offense at the time. I don't know what happened to the liquor after it was transported.

My dad drank — morning, noon and night; he had an insatiable appetite for alcohol. I don't recall Dad's drinking before I was nine or ten years old. However, once I became aware of his habit, it became something I will never forget. I learned to live with it, and forgive him, but I won't ever forget the misery that his alcohol abuse caused.

Dad and several of his friends got caught with illegal bootleg, and all were sent to a Federal prison in South Carolina for six months. I don't remember the name of the city, but I do have the faintest memory of us traveling to see him, and standing outside a building that was near an airport. I remember this because there were so many planes taking off and landing. I'd never seen airplanes before! That's all I remember — the airplanes.

My dad, Trent Howerton (circa 1951)

Mom later told us that Dad would write to her to ask for money for cigarettes and other personal items. She didn't like it that he asked for money when she had very little. We were poor before this happened, and even poorer afterwards. While Dad was incarcerated, my family pretty much lived on beans and potatoes, and whatever we could grow in the garden. Mom applied and was approved for welfare benefits. We didn't get much, but it helped with some of the household expenses. There were four of us boys, and honestly, I don't know how Mom made it through all this.

In winter we had a fuel oil stove in the living room and a small wood stove in the kitchen. I remember us kids trampling through snow looking for fallen tree limbs so we'd have something to put in the wood stove for heat. Occasionally a relative or neighbor would buy us a truck load of what we called *slab sides*, which was part of a tree that had been cut with the bark on one side and smooth on the other. We'd have to saw them into small pieces in order to get them in the wood stove. I remember one particular instance when we got a truck load of this wood and it was soaked from rain that day. When we put the wood in the heater the fire almost went out. I remember sawing wood in the cold until my hands and feet were numb. It was something we had to do every day if we wanted to keep warm.

Sometimes a friend or neighbor would cut down a nearby tree and cut it up into small blocks. We'd take a maul with an iron wedge and bust up the blocks of wood so they'd fit in the small heater. We'd only run the oil stove on really cold days. At night we could put an extra quilt on the bed to stay warm. Our house had no insulation and was not sealed very well around the windows, so when the winter wind blew hard enough you could feel the cold air coming in through cracks around the window sills.

Some days the temperature would drop into the teens or below. The ground would freeze solid and the water pipes under the house would freeze, and sometimes burst! We'd have to get the pipes repaired and wrap them in heat tape, or they'd just freeze and burst again during the next cold spell. Now that I think back, the old tobacco barn probably was better insulated than our house, and warmer too!

Dad came home after six months. I remember he brought home a wallet and a handbag that he had made out of the foil and plastic wrappers of cigarette packs. The workmanship was very colorful and artistic, but I have no idea what happened to that wallet and handbag. I later learned that this craft is called *prison art*. If I know Mom, she probably got rid of them because they reminded her of how Dad wanted money for cigarettes, money a struggling family couldn't afford to send.

Dad continued to drink after returning from prison, sometimes so heavily that we had to help him get in bed to sleep it off. We had an outside well house where Dad stored his bootleg liquor. He would go outside and hang around the well house, a structure with a roof and sides, just big enough to cover the well pump and pipes. In the wintertime, we had to run an electric cord with a light bulb on the end to the well house, and position it near the pipe that came out of the well itself. Otherwise, those pipes would freeze.

On several occasions, I saw Dad poke his head out from the back of the well house to see if anyone was watching him. He'd then take a big swig from the liquor jar and come back inside the house. He wasn't fooling anyone. We could smell the alcohol on his breath. It was almost strong enough to get a small child intoxicated! He would repeat this scenario over and over until he finished off a pint jar. By then he had usually gotten belligerent and wanted to be confrontational. He ended up losing his job at the gas station, so us kids would do odd jobs and pitch in whenever we could.

There were times Dad would go to country dances, stay out all night, and then come home early in the morning, just as intoxicated as he was when he left. I remember one time being at the table for supper, and one of us kids spoke out of turn. He'd usually wallop us on the butt for this type of offence, but this time Dad stood up and turned the table upside down on the floor. Food and dishes went flying everywhere! My two younger brothers were crying. Mom was crying and pleading with him to stop. Dad stormed out of the house to get more to drink. We cleaned up the mess and tried to make sense of it all, but there wasn't any sense to make of it. Just madness brought on by overindulgence in alcohol. Can you imagine young children, ages nine, eleven, and thirteen having to deal with this behavior? We were afraid of our own dad, someone who was supposed to be there to love, support and protect us. The only thing we could do is steer clear of him until he sobered up.

I remember another time when Dad got furious with us kids because we were laughing and talking, and he grabbed a package of frozen hamburger out of the freezer and slammed it through the window of the back door. A friend came by the next day and asked what had happened. Dad told him that the kids hit a softball through the glass.

There were other times when Dad would get angry and argue back and forth with Mom. Sometimes I'd wish that he'd just go anywhere and leave us alone. It would get so bad that I'd often go outside to get away from the confusion. If it happened to be wintertime, I'd stand next to the house to be out of the cold wind. I'd go back inside when things had settled down.

My oldest brother (Richard) did not get along with Dad. During conflicts, Richard would end up leaving the house to stay with friends. We never knew where Richard went, or whom he was with. I never really felt close to my brother because he was always gone. He was only fifteen at the height of Dad's drinking. Richard leaving the house only added to Mom's misery; she never knew where he was going, or if he was safe. When my brother would come back the next day, he and Dad would always have a confrontation, usually in the front yard, in front of all the neighbors and passersby on the street. I remember Dad chasing Richard with a baseball bat, and my brother turning, picking up rocks and tossing them back at him. This ugliness went on for a few years. The two never reconciled. When my brother became an adult, he basically just tolerated Dad.

My brother Richard and my grandpa Newton (circa 1961) at Grandpa's house. His old smokehouse is in the background.

I remember when we were growing tobacco, Dad would come into our bedroom at 6:00 a.m. and yell at us to get up. There was work to be done in the tobacco fields, at the barn and at the pack house. If we didn't get up, he'd come back and drag the covers off of us and yell some more. I usually got up the first time he came in the bedroom because I didn't want things to escalate. I remember him saying, "Don't let me come in here again." I'd get up and make myself eggs, toast, and have a slice of tomato and a cup of coffee. Not much for a boy of thirteen to eat until noon. I remember being really nervous and nauseous all the time, not knowing if he was in an okay mood, or if he was going to yell at us.

Sometimes the drinking and the yelling would get so unbearable that Mom, my two younger brothers and myself would go to Grandma's house down the road. We'd come back in the morning when Dad had sobered up. I remember Mom commenting about Dad's drinking quite often. She'd tell him, "You get drunk to tell your sober thoughts." That would just make him even angrier. Us kids would tell her not to provoke him, just let him go to bed and sleep it off.

Some people get very angry when they drink. I guess the repressed thoughts and inhibitions come out then. Then there are people who drink and become depressed and withdrawn. Still others get happy when they drink. I don't drink as much as I used to because of health reasons, but when I did, I enjoyed myself, especially if there was a crowd. My two younger brothers never drank very much. My oldest brother drank but never displayed a temper like Dad.

Dad worked at J.P. Stevens, the local textile mill. Sometimes when he was still drinking, he would go in to work mildly inebriated. We referred to this as being *half lit*. Somehow, he eluded being caught at work. Or maybe his boss knew about it and overlooked it. Dad would end up spending most of his paycheck on booze, and Mom would have to figure out how to manage on little, or no money.

There was one time when we were farming, and Dad ran up a beer tab at the nearby country store. When we sold our tobacco, the store owner came to our house and told Mom that the bill was something like $600. She paid store owner out of money we had gotten from selling the crop. I remember her telling the store owner not to ever let Dad have any more beer *on time*, or on a charge account. She told the store owner that he would not get paid if he did so. To my knowledge, Dad never charged anymore beer at that store.

Then there were the many times that Dad would go out with his buddies. We'd be fast asleep and he'd come stumbling into the house at 2:00 a.m. with his friends. I had gotten a small Magnus chord organ for Christmas when I was about eleven years old, and Dad would drag me out of bed and ask me to play *On Top of Old Smoky*.

Dad was never satisfied with just one rendition. He would lean over my shoulder and say, "Play it one more time!" I could smell the putrid odor of alcohol breath blowing over my neck and down my back. I had to play that song over and over until Mom told him that we all needed to go to bed, and that his friends had to leave. If we were lucky, he would relent, only to start all over the next day. I ended up despising that song! I wish that he had made a different request. Sometimes I think about it, and that song gets stuck in my mind, playing over and over again.

Old Magnus chord organ (circa 1965)

(A brief side note: *On Top of Old Smoky* is a traditional folksong of the Appalachian Mountains, originally brought over to America by English, Irish and Scottish immigrants).

Dad drank so much that he got bleeding ulcers. On two occasions I remember Mom having to call emergency personnel. In the 1960s and 1970s they were referred to as the rescue squad. Dad was taken to the hospital each time where he spent more than a week recuperating. When he got home, he'd start drinking all over again. The second time he was hospitalized, he almost died. After that, he gave up alcohol. This was in 1972, around the time that I graduated from high school. He never went to counseling or Alcoholics Anonymous. He just quit, cold turkey. He started going to church with Mom and genuinely tried to make a change in his behavior. The pressure we felt as kids sort of dissipated, but the memory of his bad behavior, and the loss of our childhood lingered for many years.

In spite of the alcohol problem, Dad was very savvy when it came to raising tobacco. He knew all the ins and outs: how to grow the plants from seed, how to prepare the land for planting, how to use tractors and other farm equipment, when to break off the flowers from the plants, how to tell when the leaves were ripe for picking, how to cure a barn full of green tobacco from the field.

My dad Willie and his Farmall tractor (circa 2008)

Dad was also great at raising a garden, and he loved to use his tractors to cultivate it. He took pride in everything he grew, especially tomatoes! Dad and I worked at J.P. Stevens together, and I remember him bringing fresh tomatoes to work to give out to friends. Everyone who knew Dad admired his garden. His coworkers and friends in the community had a lot of respect for him. And in later years, I too had respect for him, and the changes he had made. We became closer than we had ever been.

Cleanliness versus Sports

When I took a writing class at Cal State Fullerton in 1998 we read from a textbook of short stories and essays. One of the essays, written by Dave Barry, compared the different outlooks women and men have on two subjects: cleanliness and sports. In a joking manner, Dave Barry suggests that the differences are biological in nature. He states that:

> a hormonal secretion takes place in women that enables them to see dirt that men cannot see, and that men are physically able to actually feel the World Series television and radio broadcast rays zinging through the air, penetrating right into our bodies. (Barry, Dave, "Batting Clean-Up and Striking Out," *Dave Barry's Greatest Hits*, 1988).

Though these claims are not to be taken seriously, we all know the stereotype that women care more about cleaning than men, and men care more about sports than women. Although it is debatable how much, if any, truth forms the basis of any stereotype, I do know that my mom and dad fit these stereotypes to a tee.

My parents were married for sixty-four years. Mom was a simple woman; she was born poor and married a poor man. He expected her to do everything for him, and everything for the four boys he fathered. At the time, this was her station in life.

My dad Willie (circa early 2000s)

In my early teens my dad tended a small tobacco farm. Everyone in the family was expected to work in the fields, including my mom. She was up at four o'clock making breakfast and getting us ready for the day. Not only did she fix our meals, she came to work with us, standing shoulder to shoulder, never complaining about the hard work she faced. When it was time to go home, we all collapsed onto the sofa, exhausted from the day's work. Mom didn't stop. She had to prepare our dinner, do the laundry, and clean; she was a victim in the marriage. However, sometime in the mid to late 1970s, Mom put her foot down and told Dad that he could continue to farm by himself if he liked, but neither she nor the kids would be involved in it anymore. Dad threw a tantrum, but he knew he was overruled by the majority this time! The tobacco allotment that my grandparents owned was then sold to my dad's brother Owen, and we no longer farmed tobacco.

We all needed to escape the pressures of everyday life, and Dad was no exception. Dad loved sports. His method of escape was to watch car races on television. One Sunday our family had all gotten together for dinner. My mom and my two sisters-in-law were sitting at the kitchen table, talking about some local news story. It was not a conversation that would change the world; it was more to pass the time than anything else.

Dad yelled in an unforgiving voice, "Could everyone please stop talking? I want to watch the Daytona 500!"

Silence fell over the room, like the calm before a storm. Even the family dog, Bengie, retreated to a less conspicuous corner of the room. Not wanting to detract from the proceedings, he too became a silent observer.

The television's volume was four decibels above normal listening range. The sound of cars zooming around the track was deafening! I wondered what pleasure could be gotten from watching thirty cars go in a circle for three hours! I suppose it was the occasional crash that created the excitement — cars exploding, metal flying, bodies breaking.

Mom said, "Can you please turn the volume down a little?"

"Yeah sure, if everyone's finished talking, I'll turn it down," he growled.

His eyes were fixed on the screen, not noticing my mom as she went about her mundane duties. He had become an extension of the television. He was locked on target. The countdown to the finish line had begun; only ten more laps to go. Bombs dropping in the backyard would not have moved Dad from his chair!

"Dinner's ready," Mom casually announced, not wanting to interrupt the goings-on.

Everyone sat at the kitchen table when they came to visit. Mom was a great cook! She would get a little annoyed with us though, especially if there was a big crowd at the house for Sunday dinner, and everybody was sitting around the kitchen table in her way. Eventually she'd tell us to go into the living room so she could cook.

"There's only twenty more minutes left in the race. I want to see the finish," Dad complained. "It's going to be very close. I think our hometown favorite is going to win."

We all sat there — my brothers, my mom and my sisters-in-law, unable to speak. We were waiting for some announcement that would allow us to resume our normal conversation. We were frozen in time.

"Oh no, Gordon lost," Dad said with disgust. "This race wasn't worth watching!"

He sprang to his feet as if struck by lightning. Five minutes earlier he had been slumped in his chair staring, hypnotized by the circling cars. We could have taken him for dead! On several occasions, I had caught him napping during the race; I couldn't figure out which was louder, his snoring or the cars!

"Let's eat," he said, as we all scrambled to the table.

"I'm sorry but dinner is cold," Mom replied. "You spent too much time watching the race."

"Can't you heat it up again?"

"No, I've done that too many times."

As she left the room, I noticed that Mom had tears in her eyes. I followed her outside to see if I could console her in some way. I understood the situation, and I had always tried to help Mom through the difficult times. After all, she was a wife, and during this time, wives were expected to do everything.

I remember in the late 1960s Mom had to have surgery; it was the only time she had a good rest! She was in the hospital for about a week, so I tried, to no avail, to keep the house somewhat neat. I also did the cooking, but I got complaints about the food. Let's face it — it wasn't as good as Mom's! When she came home, the house was in a shambles. It looked as if a tornado had touched down, but only long enough to mix the contents into unorganized heaps. My mom had always held the family and the house together, but the minute she left, everything fell apart. There was no one there to keep it organized.

Dad did not like housework. His idea of organization was to move the dirt from one room to another, or from one corner to another. Dave Barry states in his essay that "men don't generally notice it [dirt] until it forms clumps large enough to support agriculture." Dad's generation considered housework to be a woman's job. Men should be allowed to watch their favorite sports shows while their wives wait on them hand and foot. That's exactly what she did. She bought all his clothes and altered them if needed. She even laid out his clothes for each day, because he would have a hard time finding anything.

Dad's outlook did change a little over the years, and he'd occasionally help some with the garden, and go to church with Mom, or take her out to get ice cream. I noticed that Mom watched a couple of races with him, and on other occasions, other sports programs. He never really helped with the housework, but did things outside, like mowing the yard and keeping the garden clean of weeds.

The stereotypes described in the Dave Barry essay are still evident in society today, but attitudes are changing. A spirit of cooperation is replacing the stereotypes, as my parents' case demonstrated.

A Better Perspective

Over the years, things got somewhat better; however, there was the lingering animosity that we all felt for being deprived of our childhood, forced to become older and more mature at an early age. And then there was the way Mom was treated. Us kids were fiercely defensive of her, and tried numerous times to intervene when Dad would become combative. Sometimes he'd push us out of the way, but we'd stand between them again. One occasion that stands out in my mind was when we had all gone to bed one night and Dad started arguing with Mom. He was so angry that he pushed her out of bed and she hit her head on the window sill by the bed. We all jumped out of bed and ran to her rescue, but she just told us she was okay, and for us to go back to bed. Situations like this terrified us and created even more of a rift between us kids and Dad.

To this day, my two surviving brothers sometimes talk about all of the chaos we endured. On top of all this, I had my own feelings to deal with. I knew I did not want to stay in a small town and struggle to make ends meet. At the same time, I worried about how Mom would be treated without any of her kids living there. However, I needed to find my own way and not have to conform to other people's ideas of where I should work, who I should be friends with or how I should conduct my life. My dad would make disparaging remarks about most of my friends that came to visit, even friends we all grew up with. It was controlling behavior and it hurt, but I kept forging ahead, hoping that one day I would leave all the chaos behind.

Mom passed away in 2014, Dad in 2016. Thinking back on how all this played out, I now believe that I have a better understanding of why Dad acted the way he did. I'm not a psychologist, but I do have insight into family relationships from being a participant, and from my twenty-year career as a Social Worker.

This is how I see it. My dad lost his dad in a car accident in 1940. Grandpa Howerton was only forty-one years old, and my grandma had eight children at the time. Dad's youngest brother was an infant. Grandma had to go and live with one of her brothers, and bring all the children with her. My dad did not have a father role model, and from what I know about the family, he had to work, doing whatever he could to help support the family. He was only ten years old when Grandpa died. He never knew how to raise a family because he never had a father figure to look up to, someone who could teach him how to raise a family. Dad resented his predicament, so he drank. And when he drank, he would direct all of this animosity toward Mom and us kids. I tell this to my brothers and try to get them to understand, and to let go of bad feelings. I tell them it doesn't help to hold that resentment inside, and that it doesn't change the facts.

Aunt Thelma

My aunt Thelma was a character in every sense of the word! I'd say she was a bit eccentric! She was the middle child in my grandparents' family, and my mom's younger sister. Thelma and my mom got married the same day, in 1950; Thelma was seventeen, Mom was twenty-one. Thelma did not want to be left at home. Their youngest sister (Aunt Laura) was only four years old, and their only brother (Uncle Crawley) was about eleven. My dad (Trent) and Thelma's husband (Andrew) were first cousins, and hung around together.

I remember Mom telling me years later, when I was old enough to understand, that Andrew beat my aunt every time she drove their car, no matter where she went. I guess he thought she was fooling around with someone else. Mom related to me that on one occasion she heard my aunt crying, so Mom walked over to her house (they lived next door to each other) to see what was going on. Her husband had hit her with a frying pan and was slapping her around! Mom asked him to stop, and Andrew told my mom that if she didn't leave, he would hit her too!

Aunt Thelma gave birth to a girl and a boy. One was stillborn and the other one was born prematurely and passed away after a few days. There is no doubt in my mind that the domestic violence was the cause of these deaths. Nothing was ever done about it. Thelma never reported it; she was afraid of even worse things happening to her if she were to do so. Remember, this was in the 1950s, and domestic violence, especially in sparsely populated rural areas of the country, was common-place. Women had to make the best of a bad situation.

Eventually Aunt Thelma got out of this relationship, divorced Andrew and started dating another man (Riley) who was a lot kinder to her.

My aunt related to me that on one occasion, she and Riley (her fiancée at the time) were sitting in his car in my grandmother's driveway when her first husband, Andrew, drove up and had a confrontation with her future husband. As the story goes, Andrew was very combative and Riley took a hand gun out of the glove box and shot Andrew in the temple. He survived the shooting, had a metal plate placed over his skull and lived a normal life after that, with only a few impediments. I believe the incident was deemed self-defense. Some years later, Andrew passed away in a car accident.

Even though Riley was good to her, I don't think Thelma ever really loved him like she did Andrew. After Thelma and Riley married, they moved out of Halifax County and relocated to Richmond. They bought a gas station and repair shop, built a new home, and made a great living for themselves, but Thelma never really seemed happy to me.

As a young teen, I became close to my aunt. Starting when I was fourteen, I would ride the Greyhound bus during the summer from South Boston to Richmond, one hundred and twenty miles, to see her. This was usually when we had a short break in the summer, just before tobacco harvesting started. I would stay a few weeks unless I was needed for work at home. We'd take trips to the beach, go out shopping and to dinner. For the most part, it was a very enjoyable and carefree time in my life.

Aunt Thelma loved convertible cars. I remember when she ordered a 1970 Dodge, Coronet 500 from the factory. It was purple with a black convertible top! We would cruise up and down streets way too fast, sometimes almost a hundred miles per hour! We got pulled over once by a State Police officer. She tried to talk her way out of a ticket, but got one anyway!

My aunt Thelma (circa mid-1950s)

Thelma was unhappy in her second marriage, and started to drink. I remember loud arguments between her and Riley, and remember feeling like I just wanted to get out of there and go home. I had seen enough of drinking with my dad's situation. On one occasion we were driving around and she decided to stop at a bar for a drink. So here we were in this redneck bar in Richmond. She's having whiskey sour's and I'm having one coke after another. All of a sudden there was a commotion in the back of the bar. Two men were fighting. I saw one person pull out a gun, so I took off for the exit. Guns have always scared me. Even when all my friends were hunting and trying to get me to go with them, I never would. I've never owned a gun. My aunt came running out behind me, screaming, "where's my nephew!" We left and I told her I'd never come to visit her anymore if she ever decided to take me to a bar again.

When I was able to drive, and after I had bought a car, I drove Mom, Aunt Laura and Grandmother to see Aunt Thelma and Uncle Riley many times. I remember on one occasion, in March 1979, I decided to take a quick weekend trip to see them by myself. I had been working in the textile mill for two years by then, and I had to be back for work at midnight on Sunday, so I decided to leave on a Saturday morning and return early Sunday afternoon.

After hearing the weather forecast early Sunday morning, I decided to return to South Boston right after breakfast. The weathermen were saying that snow was headed north from the Deep South. What I didn't know was that it had already arrived in the eastern outskirts of the city. I was headed west, so I thought maybe I would be okay. About thirty minutes into my drive home, I ran smack into the middle of one of the worst blizzards we had ever experienced! We had no cell phones then, and there was only one route on which to get home. There were no service stations or convenience stores. Had my car stalled out, I would have had to walk to the nearest home and hope someone would help me. The further I drove, the harder it snowed.

The temperature dropped to ten degrees! In that area of Virginia, there are two lanes going east and two going west, divided by a grassy median. When the snow covered the four lanes and the grass, it was a vast, stark, flat field of snow. I could barely see due to the angle at which the wind was blowing the snow. I couldn't even tell where the road was anymore! I happened to end up behind an eighteen-wheeler, so I followed in its tire tracks, driving about thirty miles per hour the entire one hundred and twenty miles! A two-and-a-half-hour trip turned into almost six hours! I made it to a gas station within three miles of where I lived when my car stalled. I found out later that the ignition points completely fused due to overheating.

We ended up with over three feet of snow at the end of that March, and our spring planting season was delayed. I never traveled anywhere again if a storm was in the forecast!

I did visit my aunt and uncle many times after that (as long as snow wasn't predicted). What I liked the most about Aunt Thelma was that we could all be sitting around talking and she would usually find something in the conversation to laugh about. Thelma's contagious laughter spread throughout the room and soon everyone was laughing! Sometimes we didn't even know what we were laughing about! It is said that laughter is the best medicine. I miss that spontaneous laughter, and that is what I loved about her the most.

Even though they didn't get along, my aunt and uncle stayed together until Aunt Thelma passed away in 2011; my uncle died a few years later.

Putting Down Roots

In the mid-1980s I began to get weary of working in a textile mill. I had been working for J.P. Stevens for about nine years at that point. Since I was seemingly locked into a dead-end position with virtually no chance to move up to a better job, I decided to return to school. At the time, there were a few college-level courses being offered at the local high school in conjunction with some of the colleges in the area. The Community College that I had attended several years earlier was too far to drive to while working full-time. I opted to just take a class here and there and try and build on the course work I had completed years earlier.

I started taking prerequisites for a business degree. Between 1986 and 1990 I only completed four or five classes. In 1986 I purchased an old dilapidated farmhouse (built in 1926) and fifteen acres of wooded land. I had resigned myself to the fact that I would probably be a career textile worker, so the house was a way to establish roots in the community. The house I bought was in a terrible state of disrepair. My family, especially my youngest brother who is a carpenter, volunteered to help me get the house in livable condition.

We worked on this house for well over three years. My brother built an entirely new kitchen and repaired the bathroom. We painted and sanded floors, and another brother fixed the plumbing and wiring. My parents helped with the yard and landscaping. In early 1989 the house was finally livable. I wanted to be on my own, but close enough to see my family. This house was only two doors down from my parents' house. Maybe it was too close! In retrospect, I probably should never have bought that house.

As I mentioned earlier in my story, I knew from an early age that I wanted to leave my hometown. During my teen years and throughout my twenties I would go out on arranged dates with women — none of my choosing though. My friends pushed me, my family encouraged me, and I know that they wanted me to put down roots there, but I had little or no interest in doing so. I wanted to make a clean break, find a better job and make a new life for myself. Living in a small town for a lot of people is ideal, but not when a person limits himself to that one area and never ventures outside of it. This is what my ancestors did, and it's what most of my current family has done, but it was just not for me.

The Magazine Ad

I subscribed to a national magazine in 1989, the same year that I finished renovating my farm house. In magazines, such as *The Advocate* or *New York Magazine*, people would place personal ads for companionship, pen pals or serious relationships. Cell phones and computers were not yet a part of mainstream communication, so there really wasn't any other way to meet new people.

I took out a small ad stating that I was looking for new friends. After a few weeks, I started receiving responses, almost on a daily basis. I rented a post office box so I could keep everything private. In the 1980s in my part of rural Virginia, everyone knew everyone else's comings and goings. Also, this was the time when AIDS was prevalent and people across the country were dying in large numbers. At the time I was primarily looking for someone to hang out with, but in the back of my mind, I was thinking that maybe I could get into a relationship and we could live in my newly-renovated house. Looking back, I think that would have been too difficult to manage, given the fact that I was not all that motivated to stay in a small town. I was also hopeful that in meeting new people I could form networks, and at least find a better job.

Many of the letters I received were from prison inmates. Some wanted me to visit them, some asked for money, but I never answered any of their letters. I answered a couple of other letters and received nice responses. One gentleman (John) lived in Richmond, Virginia and the other one lived in a small town called Farmville, Virginia. We wrote back and forth a couple of times and I drove to Richmond one Saturday and had lunch at John's house. He was a nice person who worked in accounting for a company, but we never seemed to find common ground as friends. I continued to correspond with him for several years after that. He eventually met someone, established a relationship and moved to Florida.

The other person's name was Adam. He was, and still is, a store owner. I met him in his hometown and we drove to Richmond, had dinner and went to a local bar. This was my first time experiencing the night life! Adam was about ten years younger than me and he was more interested in hanging out with a younger crowd. So, we drove back to Farmville and I drove home. I think it was like 4:00 a.m. when I got home. We corresponded for a number of years afterwards, and eventually lost touch. Recently, after more than twenty-five years, I saw him on Facebook and we exchanged a brief hello and updates on our lives. He didn't seem interested in renewing the friendship.

A California Connection

In November 1989 I saw a small ad in the magazine I subscribed to, *The Advocate*, stating that the person was looking for friends and a possible relationship. The person lived in California though. His name was Brian. The furthest that I had been away from home was Florida, but the idea of establishing a friendship in California was intriguing to me. I was also interested in finding employment in another area.

Brian and I corresponded by mail and phone, off and on for about six months. Long distance calls were billed by the minute back then, and I remember telephone bills in the hundreds of dollars! Brian lived with his two sisters in a two-bedroom apartment. I expressed an interest in visiting Southern California, so around the middle of May 1990, I purchased airfare to Los Angeles. At that time, I did not have a computer, so I had to drive to the next city over from South Boston to purchase a ticket at a ticket agency.

Our first meeting was somewhat awkward. For a short while we found it a bit more difficult to talk in person than on the phone. But we soon warmed up to each other. It was also my first time flying, and I was nervous and a bit scared. I remember thinking, "What if no one shows to pick me up at the airport? What will I do then?" But Brian was there. He gave me a warm and reassuring hug. As he drove us to Orange County, I remember thinking that Southern California was very crowded (and still is).

Brian and I spent the next two weeks getting better acquainted. He was easy to talk to and we had long discussions about our lives and backgrounds. We shared with each other our mutual hopes, dreams and desires. A strong bond was formed, and we became very close.

Brian, Kitty and me early 2000s

I was able to see some of the sights while visiting, including Disneyland and the San Diego Zoo. Brian took me to see the Joffrey Ballet perform *Romeo and Juliet* at the Los Angeles Music Center. This was the first time that I had seen any type of performing arts. It was magical!

At the end of the two weeks, I had a long discussion with Brian, and we decided that I would move to Southern California and look for work. I flew back home to Virginia and had a serious discussion with my family. I would be moving soon. Everyone was kind of silent about the issue. I guess it was quite a shock! Some family members thought I was nuts to leave. I tried my best to reassure everyone that I'd be okay. After all, I was an adult and adults make decisions. Whether or not those decisions turn out well has a lot to do with motivation. And I was motivated!

I returned to J.P. Stevens, the textile factory where I had been working for thirteen years. It was around the first of June, 1990. I remember working for about a week while pondering my decision. Was this the right decision? As time passed, and I got back into the groove of work, I realized just how much I disliked what I was doing. There wasn't much of a future there.

Around the second week of June, I gave my two-week notice. Everyone at work was completely shocked when I told them what my plans were. Co-workers told me that life was too fast in California. A family member stated that, "You'll be back in less than six months." It seemed like people were trying to dissuade me from leaving. I wondered if somehow those people were trying to make sense of their own situation and maybe they'd feel better if they convinced me to stay. But my mind was made up.

Brian flew out to Virgina during the week of the fourth of July, 1990. I had already shipped most of my possessions out to Orange County, CA where I would be living with my three friends while looking for work. I listed my house for sale and we packed my remaining items in my 1981 Mustang and took Interstate 40 all the way out to California. Most of the country we saw was from the car window though, stopping only to rest and get food and gas.

It was hard to say goodbye to friends and family. Mom cried when I left, and she cried years later. Every time I flew out to see her and Dad and other family members she would cry when I left to go back to California. I don't think she ever got used to the fact that I had moved. I was the last of four siblings to leave home, and had been the one who helped my parents the most with whatever they needed.

First Jobs

When Brian and I made it back to Orange County, I started looking for a job right away. I applied for a position at a real estate company working in their mailroom. I remember getting on an elevator to go up to the 14th floor for my interview and an earthquake hit! I could feel the building swaying and had the scary thought that the building might come tumbling down and end my California experience prematurely! I had flashbacks of working in our tobacco field with my brothers and my mom, and wondered aloud, "How could this be happening?" People were holding on to each other. I had never experienced an earthquake, so I did not know what to expect. After about twenty seconds, the swaying stopped and I went to my interview. My flashbacks subsided. About a week later I received a call that I was hired!

Working in the mailroom was grueling. There were non-stop requests from real estate agents. I had about three days training and was on my own after that. I was trying to adapt to a new job, life in a crowded environment, getting used to how people talked, and of course, traffic. To be honest, it was a nerve-racking time for me. In a small town, the traffic was very slow and sparse, and life moved at a much slower pace. In California it was exactly the opposite. I had no experience in an office setting, except for a few weeks at my previous job in Virginia. Eventually I got the hang of it, but I felt it wasn't something I wanted to do long-term.

I kept looking for other positions, and found one at an insurance company (Transamerica) across the street from where I was working. The company hired me and about six other people, and trained all of us for insurance accounting. While working there, the company encouraged me to go to school and take some accounting courses, which I did. I got a couple of raises and some good experience to use later.

In 1992 I decided to re-enter college and enrolled at a local school, Coastline Community College. At the time there was no campus, only an administration building and a book store. I took Liberal Arts plus twelve units of accounting. The classes were offered through video that you could access on educational TV, or pick up a VHS copy at the college bookstore. Also, a limited number of classes were offered after hours at local high schools, elementary schools and community centers. There was also a course of study called *weekend college*. Classes were held each Friday from 6:00 p.m. until 10:00 p.m., and all day on Saturdays for four weeks. I only took a few of those type of classes because it was too intense for someone working forty hours a week. For the video classes, a student only had to go to a physical location to take exams.

Being a full-time working adult and a college student, I was asked to be a spokesperson for the school. I accepted and was featured in a newspaper advertisement promoting the school as a great place for working adults. The convenience of watching a class on TV, taking tests at home and mailing in a scantron to the school was really helpful for working adults.

Unfortunately, Transamerica relocated to Texas in 1993 and did not offer anyone a transfer, so I was looking for work again. I applied for another accounting job at Continental Insurance and was hired a few months after leaving Transamerica. The work was very similar and I enjoyed my duties.

The company sent me to Chicago and to Dallas for training. I gladly went because it was not only an opportunity to learn a new job, but also to travel, which I loved. After a few years with this company, there was a buy-out in 1996 and I was again faced with unemployment. I began searching for work again and found employment with a company that manufactured insulation products for the airline industry. What was interesting about this job is that twice a year a group of employees had to travel to Mexico to do inventory at the manufacturing plant. So again, I got to travel to places I had never been. This company eventually starting downsizing in 1998 and I was laid off. I figured I'd go ahead and start looking for a new job, but this time I tried to focus on employment that would be long-term instead of just taking any job.

Me in 1999, starting my career as a Social Worker

Continuing My Education

In 1996 I decided to go for a Bachelor's Degree and enrolled in the Sociology program at Cal-State University, Fullerton, CA. I had looked at the possibility of getting a government job, particularly in the Social Services field, but I didn't have the required credits in Social Science. When I became a student at the university, I worked for temporary agencies for a few years, but wasn't interested in going full-time in any of those jobs. Working for agencies paid the bills, and that was the important thing. In 1998, while still attending college, I applied and was hired for a limited term job in the University's Accounting Department. I remained there for the one-year term until I graduated.

The best part of working at the university was that I could leave work and walk across campus to my classes! For the first two years of taking classes at Cal State Fullerton I worked ten miles away from campus, so I left work at 5:00 p.m. and drove directly to school where I grabbed a bite to eat before my 6:30 p.m. class started. The days were long, and I remember getting home after 10:00 p.m. each night, having to try and do homework and get a decent night's sleep before starting all over again the next day. This new arrangement was so much easier.

Obtaining my Bachelor's Degree in Sociology from Cal State Fullerton was a huge accomplishment. I was so proud of myself. I had first started taking college classes in 1972, and it only took me 27 years to finally get my degree! Perseverance pays off.

Graduation day was a big event. James Cameron (CSUF alum and director of the movie *Titanic)* was the commencement speaker. Since I was president of the Fullerton chapter of Alpha Kappa Delta, the honor society for Sociology students, I gave a speech at the luncheon for Sociology graduates that was held after commencement. I was a bit nervous, but Brian told me I did a terrific job.

About a month after graduation, I applied for a Social Worker position with the County of Orange and was hired. I went through a three-month training class in which I learned Medi-Cal (Medicaid in all other states) procedures and coding. I was then transferred to one of the Social Services regions in the county to begin working with clients ensuring that their benefits were issued in a timely manner. I was assigned a caseload of approximately 300 clients.

After one year I was promoted to Ongoing Services Worker. Cases were assigned to me from the initial intake process. This job involved working with clients to maintain, on an ongoing basis, the cash aid, food stamps and Medi-Cal benefits on their cases. My caseload was approximately 100 clients.

I was promoted again two years later, this time as an Initial Services Worker. In this position I would set up cash, food stamp and Medi-Cal cases during face-to-face interviews with clients. Once set up, the case was transferred to an Ongoing Services Worker. I worked this position for five years, and then took a lateral position as Case Manager.

As Case Manager, I assisted clients in locating employment, job training and education. There were many partners with Social Services who provided these services. My job was to refer the clients to these partners and provide referrals to supportive services such as child care, housing, and transportation. I also worked to remove potential barriers that clients might face as they sought employment or training.

I worked for a total of nineteen and a half years for the County of Orange, and retired in 2018. After nine years of working many different jobs in Southern California, some of which were out of basic necessity, I finally figured out that I was best suited for working with people in a helping capacity. It was a very rewarding career.

Conclusion:
The Journey Is Complete

It has been a long journey from the tobacco fields and textile mills of Southern Virginia, but it has been a productive one. When I moved to Orange County many people back home told me it could not be done, that I wouldn't survive in the fast-paced world of Southern California, and that I'd want to return home to Virginia in a few months. It took perseverance, determination, motivation and support from friends and my partner Brian to be able to make the kind of move that I made, and to make it last. In 1990 I had not heard of anyone who had uprooted their lives and moved to another city, especially clear across the country, so I'm proud of the fact that I was able to relocate and establish a good life. Nowadays, moving to new areas of the country and finding new employment is more commonplace.

When I was a teenager, I pulled tobacco plants from a plant bed, rode a mechanical planter on the back of a tractor and transplanted the plants in the field, nurturing them along the way, and giving them a chance at new life. The same can be said for me. I transplanted myself to a new environment in California and gave myself a new life, one that has provided for me for over thirty-five years now. I think back to the days of long ago when I was riding our rickety old trailer to the tobacco field, wondering if there might be something different for me. It has been quite a journey.

Living here has given me the opportunity to meet new people, both at work and away from my job. It has also given me the chance to travel, which I had always wanted to do. Brian and I became Domestic Partners in 2008 and together we have visited Mexico, Canada, the Northeastern U.S., the South, the Western states and the Midwest. We have seen a lot of historic places such as Philadelphia, Charleston, New York, and Boston. I don't have any regrets for leaving the tobacco farm and the textile mill.

In any event, the textile industry in my hometown disappeared in the early 2000s and the small farms in that area of Virginia are now practically non-existent. According to an aunt who lives in the area, there are currently about five large highly-mechanized tobacco farms remaining, several hundred acres each.

I am appreciative of the fact that living in a small town, working on a tobacco farm, and working in the textile industry instilled in me a good work ethic. These pivotal events taught me the importance of community, character, and lasting relationships. When I moved to California, I said my *farewell to farms*, but I don't want to forget, or to take any of my upbringing for granted. I cherish my small-town roots. They are an integral part of who I am. I have continued my family's legacy in agriculture, but instead of growing tobacco, I grow lots of fruits and vegetables in the backyard, and at the Orange Community Garden.

Writing this memoir has involved much thinking and reflecting upon my life. In hindsight, I can see four distinct phases: birth and childhood in Virginia, moving and adjusting to life in California, my 20-year career as a Social Worker, and my retirement. I imagine each phase similar to a theatrical performance. We all play different roles and experience various episodes throughout our lives, each ending like the conclusion of an act in a play.

Sometimes transplanting a seedling to a new location is too much of a shock, and the little plant eventually withers and dies. I am fortunate that the transplantation of my life from South Boston to Orange County has been a success. With the love and support of family and friends I continue to thrive in this new environment.

Kitty Li'l Boy in 2019

Mom's Favorite Recipes

Squash Casserole

Ingredients:
2 cups cooked yellow squash
1 cup chopped onion
3/4 stick butter (melted)
1 cup grated cheese
2 eggs (beaten)
1 cup milk
1 tsp. salt
2 cups crushed saltine crackers

Directions:
Cook squash until fork tender and mash. Add all other ingredients except eggs. Stir and add eggs last. Pour into greased baking dish. Bake at 375° for 40 minutes.

Chocolate Chess Pie

Ingredients:
1 ½ cups sugar

1 tsp. vanilla

1 tbsp. flour

2 eggs

3 tbsp. cocoa

½ cup milk

½ stick butter (melted)

Directions:
Mix sugar, flour and cocoa in a bowl. Stir out all lumps. Add eggs, butter, vanilla and milk. Beat until smooth. Bake in unbaked pie shell at 350° for 40 minutes.

Sweet Potato Pie

Ingredients:

2 cups cooked, mashed sweet potatoes

1 cup heavy cream

⅔ cup firmly packed light brown sugar

2 large eggs

1 tsp. ground cinnamon

½ tsp. ground ginger

½ tsp. ground nutmeg

¼ tsp. ground allspice

1 unbaked 9" pie shell

Directions:

Heat oven to 450°. Combine sweet potatoes, sugar, cream, eggs, cinnamon, ginger, nutmeg and allspice. Pour mixture into pie shell. Bake 10 minutes. Reduce oven temperature to 325°. Bake pie 40 minutes longer or until center is set. Cool completely on a wire rack. Serve with whipped cream if desired. 8 servings. Refrigerate leftovers.

About the Author

Douglas Howerton is a retired Social Worker who enjoys writing, gardening and travel. He volunteers with a local group that rescues cats. He lives in Southern California with Brian, his partner of thirty-four years, and their beloved cat Li'l Boy. This is Douglas's first book. He wanted to tell his story in hopes of encouraging other people who are struggling to find their identity, to take a chance and not limit themselves to one place or one job. He also wanted to stress the value of hard work, the importance of preserving one's history, and the strength of good relationships and camaraderie of close friendships. *A Farewell to Farms* takes you back to a simpler time. The journey has been long but rewarding.

www.ingramcontent.com/pod-product-compliance
Lightning Source LLC
Chambersburg PA
CBHW051148120626
46547CB00012B/987